Praise for
The Feminine Path to \

This unique book inspires and engages. Its organic weaving of personal story with creative exercises invites the reader to explore and deepen her own life path. Russell's search to become the heroine of her own life is a teaching tale. Her vulnerable struggles with single parenthood, career, addiction, sexuality and marriage reveal the universal through the individual. It's a soulful quest, aided by teachers, and informed by the discovery of her embodied feminine and wounded masculine sides. Above all, it is a story of her courageous dedication to find her true self, and to be true to the call of her destiny.

She urges the reader to discover the sacred purpose of her own life, guided by "the sound of your soul calling you to wholeness, calling you onto a journey, to remember who you really are: a spiritual being having a human experience."

Margaret Wilbur M.A., M.F.A., Jungian Analyst,
Professor Emerita School of Theater, UCLA

With transparency, candor and warmth, Colleen Russell communicates the rewards of a struggle for wholeness: spiritually, physically and emotionally. She tells her personal story with compelling honesty, and her wise counsel provides a map and courage for the journey. She worked on herself deeply, not avoiding the hard issues of guilt, shame, loss, grief, anger and abuse. She undertakes each necessary task to find the freedom to be herself and to heal the split between body/soul that so many of us experience. Russell shares the vulnerable details of her experience as an inspiring offering and includes stimulating exercises to aid the reader in her own process. She proves that it really IS possible to live in harmony with one's authentic self.

Dorothy J. Anderson, Ph.D. Professor, UCLA
Leadership Consultant, Workshop Leader, Artist.

The Feminine Path to Wholeness

The Conscious Queen

The Feminine Path to Wholeness
Becoming a Conscious Queen

Written and Illustrated by Colleen R. Russell,
M.A. Transpersonal Psychology

Self Published - Colleen R. Russell, MATP - The Artful Sage
www.theartfulsage.com

Printed in the USA

Design by Colleen R. Russell, MATP

ISBN 9-781721-866199

I dedicate this book to my seventeen-year-old self who had the courage to rise up and become the heroine of her life in the face of extreme adversity. I honor the courageous and supportive women who forged the path before me.

Rise Up

Table of
Contents

Foreword . i

Preface . iii

Introduction:
The Return of the Feminine . 1

The Third Wave • Explore Your Story

Exercise: The Cost of Freedom . 7

The Story of Me . 11

Thrown Out of the Garden • The Middle Years • Becoming a Woman
Encounters with the Patriarchy • Wearing the Scarlet Letter
A Girl Without a Dream • Leap and the Bridge will Appear • Battling Depression
Expansion • Iguana Love You Like No One Has Before-The Turning Point
Becoming the Father of My Own Experience • Signs of Change

Exercise: Gathering Your Story Elements . 27

The Unraveling . 31

Sitting in the Ashes • The Long Road to Healing • Meeting the Ski Patrol Man
Breakdown of the Body • The Call • Encounters with the Feminine
Taking Flight • Grieving and Searching • Creating a New Life • Emerging
Becoming a Facilitator/Teacher/Healer • Healing Body/Mind/Spirit
Bringing Back the Treasure • Giving Back/Creating Anew • Another Loss of Self

Exercise: Tracking Your Journey . 53

Embracing the Shadow . 57

Healing Our Mother Wounds • Awakening the Creative • Going Deeper
Encountering the Shadow • The Inner Child • Coming Home to My Body • Completion
Exercise: Accepting Yourself . 65

Healing the Wounded Masculine . 71

Removing the Patriarchal Mask • My Father • Father Church • School Authorities
Relationships • The Patriarchal Culture and Collective Mindset • Letting Go of Anger
Confronting the Critic, the Tyrant, and the Predator of the Psyche
Connecting to a Positive Masculine • The Sacred Marriage
Exercise: Understanding and Healing Your Inner Masculine . 84

Exploring Addiction . 89

Spiritually Bereft • Addiction History • Body Disconnect • The Twelve Steps
Forgiveness of Self and Others • Loving Myself Just as I Am
Exercise: Getting Honest . 97

Bridging Love and Sexuality . 101

Body-Soul Split • Sex and Marriage • Second Marriage
Another Step to Becoming Authentic • Healing the Womb • The Creative Life Source
Exercise: Inhabiting Our Bodies . 110

The Conscious Queen . 115

The Third Wave of the Feminist Movement • Awaken the Masculine • The Gift
The Labyrinth
Exercise: Standing in Your Power . 124

Afterword . 127
Glossary . 130

Art Index

The Conscious Queen	Title	All is Welcome Here	44	Blessed is She	87
Rise Up	TOC	Stepping Out	46	Tied in Knots	88
Felicity	iv	Medicine Woman	47	Night Journey	91
Anastasia	v1	The Seeker	49	Centered	93
Young Maiden	4	Lost Dreams	51	Bucket Woman	95
The Feminine Path	5	Heart Wisdom	52	Garden Devi	96
Express Your True Colors!	9	Held in Love	53	Shadow Self	97
Queen in the Making	10	Breath of Life	55	Interwoven	99
Trust the Mystree	12	Coming into Wholeness	56	Ancient Wisdom	100
Child Spirit	13	Emerging Feminine	58	Holy Vessel	102
Growing Up	15	Fully Embodied	60	Listening	106
Party Girl	17	Artist Within	61	Nature Goddess	107
Fall from Grace	18	Shaman	62	Goddess of Fertility	
Leaving Home	20	Fairy Princess	63	Abundance	109
Endings	21	Uniquely You	64	Spirit Companions	111
In Relationship	23	Lion King	70	Color-Filled	112
Working Girl	25	Individuating	72	At Home	113
Shape of Things to Come	26	Dad	73	The Artful Sage	114
The Storyteller	27	In the Arms of the Mother	76	In Full Bloom	116
Winter's Glow	30	Entering Sacred Ground	77	Sisterhood	117
Broken Hearted	33	Be Yourself	78	The Great Mother	118
Inner Wisdom	34	Be Brave	79	Standing in Her Power	119
Emerging	36	Spiritual Warrior	81	Malei	121
Listen to Your Heart	39	Co-Creator	82	Messenger of Hope	123
Loving All of Me	40	Inspired Creativity	83	Ruler of Her Kingdom	125
Pondering	41	At Your Service	84	Throne of Empowerment	128
Queen of the Night	42	Inner Masculine	86		

Prints and many originals are available for purchase on my website at
www.theartfulsage.com

Foreword

I caution the reader not to begin this book, unless you are willing to have your life changed. Absolutely read this book if you wish to enter into an authentic exploration of your unlived and unclaimed life.

The oldest recorded story of the Feminine, incised in clay tablets over five thousand years ago, is the myth of Inanna: Queen of Heaven and Earth. The Sumerians, a tribe with a highly-evolved cultural structure, metaphorically mapped the psychological changes a woman must yield to in order to claim her autonomy from the status quo. It is a story of sacrifice; of letting go of distorted faulty beliefs. It is a story of descent into the inner sanctum of soul-searching and ownership for all the choices made that are self-impeding. It teaches the profound courage that envelops our lives when we learn that "Not for me" is a complete sentence.

To read Colleen's story is to validate Inanna's story, as true today as it was five thousand years ago.

With humility and deep introspection, the story contained in these pages rings profoundly true and inexplicably freeing as the author allows herself to be revealed "stripped down and naked," and vulnerable in the face of life's harshest lessons.

Colleen is a gifted writer; whose soft voice invites us to dare to love ourselves without the chorus of critical and shaming voices we usually concede to. She teaches that until each of us is able to forgive our Self for choosing the survival tactics we embraced in the past—to accept our own humanity and forgive even when we struggle with forgetting—we are living someone else's story, not our own.

She teaches us that every woman lives her life guided by three stories: There is the external story we acquire or inherit from others. There is the inner story we believe about our Self, peopled by a myriad of teachers, critics, and comparisons. There is a deeper and wiser authentic story carried by our Soul.

As you read this book, Colleen's soul story unfolds. And the reader's own untold soul story recognizes the invitation to "come home to myself," through it.

Years ago I read a quote from that great teacher of dance, Martha Graham. She wrote:

> "There is a life force, an energy, a quickening, that is translated through you into action, and because there is only one of you through all time, this expression is unique and if you block it, it will never exist through any other medium."

The authentic Self carries that life force, quietly and relentlessly nudging each of us to stand still and take time to descend and listen to the Soul's story—to learn how to inhabit your own body and trust that you, and you alone, have the capacity to fully inhabit your own life in spite of the losses and diminishing moments...and the "what ifs."

When I read this story, I felt a sense of deep blessing. I had awakened way before dawn and read until daybreak. The pre-dawn lightly colored the bits of sky peeking through the forest in which I live. I said my morning prayers of gratitude and listened to my inner voice. It called me to go inward; as I did, I sensed a smooth descent toward an unknown destination.

As I surrendered to the image, I was infused with a knowing that did not need words: I had been awakened down, down, down to a source within that was now deeply fed by a fellow pilgrim on her own journey. And as I dropped into a deep sleep I knew that this book had opened a door I would step through organically, in its time not mine, and find yet another insight into my own "uniqueness."

Each life is a thread in a tapestry that encompasses all lives—past, present, and yet to come.

I invite you to open these pages, surrender not to the losses or disappointments of your life but to the sweet adventure of "coming home to yourself."

Paula M. Reeves, PhD
Psychotherapist, Mythographer, Author,
Women's Intuition: Unlocking the Wisdom of the Body and Heart Sense: Unlocking Your Highest Purpose and Deepest Desires

Preface

While you had a chance to live, did you become your true self?

~ Michael Meade

This book is the story of how I found the feminine path to wholeness and became a Conscious Queen. You will discover the obstacles I encountered, the teachers I met, and the wisdom and gifts I uncovered along my way.

To me, a Conscious Queen is a woman who knows who she is because she has experienced the transformative fires of initiation and has found her true self. No longer burdened by the patriarchal influence, strapped with images of unachievable perfection, consumed by addiction or obsessive/compulsive behavior, she is free to become the author of her life and the ruler of her kingdom. She has moved beyond fragmentation and into wholeness - living, creating, and embracing the union of the masculine and feminine within her.

Myths and fairy tales have been used for centuries to teach about the inner journey. Using a similar model in this book, I chose to give you a contemporary view of the journey through my personal story and my art. Although my story is different from yours, many of our challenges are the same.

I believe that you, your unique gifts, and the expression of those gifts are necessary to balance the love of power with the power of love in our modern-day culture. Your gifts and wisdom, together with women like you, are the healing salve that can heal the separation we feel from others, the sacred, and the earth.

Never before has the stage been more prepared for women to step into their power and share their unique gifts. It requires each of us to take the inner journey to confront our own power principle and inner oppressor so we can step onto that stage as fully empowered women. Truly empowered (not imitating the power principle), we are Conscious Queens who are connected to our voice, our body, and confident in our right to step onto the throne as equal partners with our internal king, restoring the value and sacredness of the feminine.

Healing is possible. You are not alone; someone understands your pain, grief, and the struggles you face. I hope my story provides inspiration to women so together we can re-unite our world.

Felicity

Deep Gratitude to:

• My son, Matthew Donahue, for being such a blessing, for his courage, love, and understanding.

• My first husband, Dennis Klausen (1943-1990), for his love, support, and encouragement.

• My second husband, Randy Russell, for his unconditional love and continuous support.

• My mom, dad, family, and friends who have loved and taught me throughout the years.

• Kathleen Jenison for all the nudges in our single parenting years.

• All the teachers who have influenced me, including but not limited to: Mr. Fraga, Paul J. Meyer, Judith Durek, Jean Houston, Natalie Rogers, Jack Canfield, Angeles Arrien, Arnie Mindell, Marcia Wieder, Jill Bodonsky, Seena Frost, Stewart Cubley, Marion Woodman and the gifted BodySoul leadership team, Berta Kuhnel, Ali Brown, Les Brown, Clarissa Pinkola Estes, Debbie Ford, Flora Bowley, Claire Zammit and Katherine Woodward Thomas, Tamara Laporte and all the teachers in the Life Book series, Shiloh Sophia, as well as the many unnamed authors whose books and teachings have given me strength, hope, and courage.

• A special thanks to Sherrye Annand, M.A. for starting me on my journey.

• Dana Smith, whose skills, love, compassion, and willingness helped me to birth this book into reality.

• Lindagail Campbell for modeling the positive mother as I wrote my book.

• All the women and men who read, encouraged, and helped to edit my book, especially Sharon Smith.

• Sandee Meade and the Scotia House Retreat Center for holding such loving space for me and so many others.

• Monastery of St. Gertrude's in Cottonwood, Idaho, for supporting me in their Artist Residency Program.

Thank you all! Without your love and support, none of this would have been possible.

We delight in the beauty of the butterfly but rarely admit the changes it has gone through to achieve that beauty.

~ Maya Angelou

Anastasia

Introduction:
The Return of the Feminine

In legend, it is said that it is the power of the feminine manifesting as love and compassion that will restore what has been dismembered to wholeness, and transform the wasteland into a garden.

~ Allan B. Chinen, <u>Waking the World</u>

I started kindergarten in 1960 when the second wave of the feminist movement was just beginning. The first wave started in 1848 and ended in 1920 with the signing of the 19th amendment which gave women the right to vote and opened the door to political, economic, and social justice for women.

Up until then, women were second-class citizens. They were expected to submit to their husbands, have babies, stay at home, and raise the children. Men were the center of authority. This model is known as the Patriarchy.

That power structure shifted somewhat during World War II, when over six million

patriarchy
noun pa·tri·ar·chy /ˈpātrēˌärkē/

Patriarchy: is a social system in which males hold primary power, predominate in roles of political leadership, moral authority, social privilege and control of property. In the domain of the family, fathers or father-figures hold authority over women and children.

women were called into the workplace. My mother was one of them. She worked at a restaurant in Oakland, California (before her nine children were born) and when we were growing up, she often told us how much she loved that time in her life. As an extrovert, she enjoyed working and socializing. When the war ended, and the men returned, she went back to caring for her home and starting a family, as did scores of other women. Their return marked the end of their careers.

By the 1950s, many women felt dissatisfied with their lot in life. After the war, they could not find employment and the promise of economic and social equality was only a dream. Most of them still felt like second-class citizens.

By 1960 the women's liberation movement was in full-swing. Their fight was for further equality, not just for women but for all people. Women wanted protection from physical abuse. They demanded more control over their bodies, especially over their reproductive rights which was made possible with the arrival of the first oral contraceptives for women in the early '60s. This possibility was a big leap in the evolution of women.

A feminist is anyone who recognizes the equality and full humanity of women and men.
~ Gloria Steinem

The '60s brought other changes as well. The National Organization for Women was formed in 1966 by Betty Friedan to ensure that both women's and civil rights were not just ideals, but realities. Gloria Steinem became the voice for women's issues. The sexual revolution was in full swing, bringing with it a sexual freedom for young women like me. It was far beyond anything my mother could have imagined.

Women boycotted the 1968 Miss America Pageant to proclaim that a woman's worth was not about beauty. By 1972, the focus was on being seen as individuals with thoughts, feelings, and lives that mattered. Women were confronting sexism in the workplace, and breaking the stereotypes of women's roles. In 1973 (the year I graduated from high school, seven months pregnant), abortions became legal and gave women even more empowerment and freedom.

Massive changes were occurring but like the earlier wave, it would take years of continued struggle to fully realize our dreams and ideals. Women found that they could have-it-all but having-it-all came with a heavy burden of responsibility. As a result of their new-found freedom, women put in an eight-to ten-hour workday in addition to still being responsible for their kids, home, and family life. This left them with no time for themselves. I remember my sisters and I saying longingly, "Gee, we wish we had a wife to take care of us!"

Even though growing up in the '60s and '70s was supposed to give us so much freedom, most of the changes barely scratched the surface of true freedom. The old order, which had been the law of the land for thousands of years, still existed within every institution and within our own individual and collective psyches. There was, and still is, much to be transformed.

Thanks to the women who have come before us, western women are now the most powerful, educated, and liberated women in recorded history. Ironically, according to Claire Zammit, PhD. and Katherine Woodward Thomas with Evolving Wisdom, there is still much discontent among us. Statistics indicate that 50% of women report they are living without a partner, 20% are on anti-depressants, 75% have an unhealthy relationship with food and their own bodies, and more than 50% continue to struggle with financial stress.

Having worked for years to have-it-all, women reach mid life only to discover that they have not lived. Exhausted and disillusioned, they find that success is not all that they thought it would be. Middle-aged women find themselves asking, "Who am I? What is my life about?" Many discover that they can no longer avoid the call to find the lost parts of themselves.

This was especially true for me. I worked years to better myself so that I could make it in a man's world. I had reached my goal of making $50,000 a year in the late 1980s, yet I was exhausted and left with a feeling that something inside of me was still unexpressed.

It was about that time (at age 35) that the well-constructed life I had created began to fall apart. Within a three-year period, my husband died, my only son left home and, with my counselor's encouragement, I gave up a seven-year career at the Yellow Pages to find my true self.

Who was I if I was no longer a wife, a mother, or an employee with a community of friends? That became the question—a question that would lead me onto a path of understanding to heal both the feminine and masculine within me. The path would ultimately help me find my voice, discover my creativity, heal my body, break free from depression and addiction, and live a life beyond my wildest dreams. I call the process of integrating and bringing the disparate parts of ourselves into wholeness and balance the feminine path to wholeness. By following this feminine path, I found my true self and experienced what true freedom means.

I hear a longing, from women both young and old, to find and live from their true selves. Many of these women are experiencing multiple transitions and do not understand that the breakdown of their old lives is the portal which leads them to the feminine path to wholeness. This pathway will uncover the freedom they seek in order to live their lives true to themselves and express the gifts they are called to give.

> *One of the greatest regrets in life is being what others would want you to be, rather than being yourself.*
> ~ Shannon L. Adler

The feminine path to wholeness is a spiritual journey which takes a person inward to reclaim parts of her *self* that have been denied, repressed, or neglected; an inward journey that brings her back to her true essence and moves her from her ego-bound self to living from her soul, or her true self. It allows her to let go of her false self and connect to the wisdom of her deepest self.

These deep inner journeys, by their very nature, take us into the land of the feminine, where we undergo the life/death/rebirth cycle - a process honored for its life-renewing capabilities. It is when a woman undergoes a metaphorical death of her old self: she lets go of the status quo so that she can step more freely into her true potential.

Young Maiden

The Third Wave

I believe individual and collective initiations into the *deep feminine* are the third wave of the feminist movement. These processes will allow us to move beyond the stereotypes of women that have been held for thousands of years. Like the phoenix rising from the ashes, women who allow themselves to be transformed through the alchemical fires that ravage their lives will rise renewed, transformed, and strengthened to live their authentic lives. As we each do this inner work, it will bring wholeness not only to ourselves, but to our families, our communities, and our world.

This book is for women who, like me, learn from stories and want to live from their authentic selves. I have done my best to be transparent because I believe that we women need to share the truths of our lives and know that we are not alone.

Iyanla Vanzant says that when you stand and share your experience in an empowered way, your story will heal you and your story will heal someone else. It is my sincere desire that you reflect on your own story and find healing. I hope too that you find the pieces you need to complete your journey so you are able to step forward to share the gifts that are meant to be lived through you.

"We are living in the age of women," said Tom Brokaw. I believe we need to step into that age now, not as a masculinized version of women, but as women who know and love ourselves and possess the courage to stand and live in our truths.

The ultimate objective of taking a spiritual journey is to metamorphose into a Divine Being. Without self-transformation, there is no freedom.

~ Guruji Krishnananda

The Feminine Path

Explore Your Story

To help you explore your story I have provided exercises at the end of each chapter. You may want to read the entire book before beginning your own exploration or you may decide to explore your story as you read each chapter. I trust you will find what works best for you.

If you choose to do the exercises, you might want to prepare as follows:

Suggested supply list:

- blank mixed-media art journal
- pen or pencil
- medium-grade watercolor paints
- glue stick
- colored markers to bring fun into your journal

- medium-grade pastel chalks, various colors
- scissors
- stack of your favorite magazines
- cards or pictures that speak to your soul
- candle/matches

Note: Many art supply stores offer coupons which can significantly reduce the cost of supplies. Items on this list are entirely optional, feel free to substitute supplies if you are unable to obtain them.

Create a *Sacred Space* for doing the exercises:

- set aside some time and find a quiet corner
- light a candle to call in the sacred
- invite your angels , guides, or spirit
- know that you can go as deep as you want or are able (this work may release strong emotions)
- honor whatever feelings arise
- stay open and loving while creating a container

for yourself and your feelings
- observe yourself as you work
- honor your path, your story, and the characters in it
- go at your own pace
- when done, close your space by blowing out your candle and by putting your journal in a place of safe keeping

Some exercises may require access to a computer, internet, and a printer. You can obtain additional resources for this book at my website. It is: www.theartfulsage.com/cqresources and the password is #ConsciousQueen

The Cost of Freedom

My favorite folk rock band growing up in the '60s was Crosby, Stills, Nash, and Young. They performed a beautiful song that honored the fathers and soldiers who had given their lives so others might be free. It was written by Stephen Stills and is titled: "Find the Cost of Freedom." The chorus goes: *Find the cost of freedom buried in the ground. Mother earth will swallow you, lay your body down.*

freedom
noun free·dom /ˈfrē-dəm/

Freedom: is the power or right to act, speak, or think as one wants without hindrance or restraint.

Death, either literally or metaphorically, is always the cost of freedom. Do you know the cost women paid for the freedom you have today? If not, I offer suggestions on the following page for further exploration.

Supplies:

- ° art journal
- ° pen or markers
- ° watercolors
- ° paintbrush

Before you begin, paint a wash of color on multiple pages in your journal and let them dry. Next, make yourself comfy and view one or more of the films listed on the next page. As you watch, pay attention to the feelings that arise in both your body and mind. Make a few notes to yourself on the painted journal pages. When done, capture any thoughts in your journal that may have emerged using images or symbols.

Honor your own courage to witness the lives of the courageous women who fought for the freedoms you have today. Write them a note thanking them for their sacred service so that you might be free.

Viewing for a rainy day:

- *The Burning Times, Women and Spirituality*, documentary, https://www.youtube.com/watch?v=YizdSL2_pMo
- *Suffragette* (2015)
- *Revolution, The Legacy of the Sixties* (2011), documentary, https://vimeo.com/22929942
- *Documentary on Women's Liberation Movement (2015)* https://www.youtube.com/watch?v=EOsLjbpHV8M
- *Vagina Monologues*, Eve Eisler (2002)
- *Thelma and Louise* (1991), A modern drama of women who are caught in the shadow-side of the patriarchy.

For the reader:

<u>Boom!: Voices of the Sixties: Personal Reflections on the '60s and Today</u>, Tom Brokaw

Express Your True Colors!

Queen in the Making

The Story of Me

My story is important not because it is mine, but because if I tell it anything like right, the chances are you will recognize that in many ways it is also yours.
~ Frederick Buechner, *Telling Secrets*

I believe I came into the world determined to be who I really am. This was my task, the mission I had chosen for this lifetime: to be true to my authentic self. Little did I know the impact of my commitment. Had I understood the complexities and the obstacles that would await me, I would have chosen another task.

The authentic self is the soul made visible.
~ Sarah Ban Breathnach

As I grew up, my mother would share stories with us about our childhood. My story was that I was the only one of her children who weighed 10 lbs. at birth, didn't suck her thumb, and was left-handed. Several of the others had started out as lefties, but she had trained them to be right-handed. I imagine she did that because during the '50s, factory machines, calculators, cash registers, even scissors were made for the right-handed person. But I was determined to be me. So even before the age of one, I willfully and successfully clung to who I was. I would follow my own path, even if it meant that I'd be the *odd duck* and not fit in with the rest of the world.

11

Sometimes my Aunt Mary (one of my mom's many sisters) brought our Irish grandmother, Mary Kate Kelly, to visit from Washington State. We barely knew our grandmother because she lived so far away; we learned about her life through stories, mostly. She emigrated from Ireland in 1913 and homesteaded with my grandfather in the wilderness near Randle, Washington, where she gave birth to and raised thirteen children without any of the modern-day amenities. We loved hearing about her life.

We especially loved Aunt Mary's visits because she had a way of making us all feel loved and appreciated. One summer I was allowed to pour the tea as they all sat outside enjoying the sun. Aunt Mary said, as she grinned adoringly at me, "There is something special about this one!" Her kind words and unconditional love were like a lifeline for me. I always felt she saw the REAL ME. I am grateful for this, because if one person in your life sees you, you will never be entirely lost.

Trust the Mystree

My life as a small child was idyllic in a way. We lived four miles outside of a small town along the southern Oregon coast. Much of my early childhood consisted of climbing trees, building forts, catching pollywogs and frogs, roaming through the forest, and looking for treasures down by the seashore. I think it is fair to say we were nature-children. We spent hours exploring the wilderness behind our home. In the late '50s and early '60s, children could still run free without their mothers worrying too much.

My parents were poor, self-reliant Irish-Catholic folk. My mother had a high school education and was the traditional stay-at-home mom who ruled her roost with an iron fist and a jovial sense of humor. My father, a quick-tempered blue-collar worker/

accountant with an eighth-grade education, could build or fix anything.

On our two-acre property, we had a milk cow which my dad milked every morning and night, usually a steer or a heifer, laying hens, a vegetable garden, fruit trees, and strawberry and raspberry patches—all organic before it was fashionable. Every fall my mom canned for weeks, as her mother had done before her, lovingly preparing food for her family for the winter ahead.

With our large family, we rarely went anywhere except to church. Thus, we grew up shy, hiding behind our mother's skirt when anybody looked at or spoke to us. During those early years we reveled in the innocence, joy, and freedom of childhood. We gave little thought to what lay beyond our little world, unless we were sleeping out under the stars. At such times we would ask, "Who are we? Where did we come from? Who do you think we would be if we had another mom or dad? Do you think there is life on other planets?" When morning came though, those questions were quickly forgotten.

Thrown Out of the Garden

Around age five, my idyllic world started to unravel as I experienced the traumas that come with being human. The first wound or trauma that I remember happened one day when I begged my dad to let me pull weeds in the garden with the older kids. He was hesitant at first (because of my age) but Mom encouraged him to let me help.

In my innocence, I pulled the new potato seedlings thinking they were weeds. My young mind couldn't distinguish the difference. When dad saw what I was doing, he exploded into a rage, cussing and yelling. He sent me out of the garden, finger pointed towards the house. When I got inside, Mom asked: "What's wrong?"

"I pulled the wrong plants and Dad told me to go to my room," I said with tears streaming down my face.

"Well, you better get in there then," she said.

I went in, hung my head low, and created a story for myself about how bad I was. I must be bad because here I was, separated from the others. I had only wanted to help, but had upset my dad instead. I'm sure the thought disappeared after a while, but the story's message remained. I began to think that I was a bad person.

The next incident took place not long after, when I was in kindergarten. Mom had a newborn and three-year-old at home, she was frequently late picking me up so I never knew when she would arrive. I'd run outside after school, art work and papers in hand, excited to show her what I'd done, but soon I was the only kid standing on the sidewalk. I'd wait and wait, and still she didn't show.

Her lateness was so chronic that my teacher bought me a stiff little doll (which I secretly hated) and we made doll clothes for her until my mother got to the school. By the time she arrived, I was in tears. She told me, "Be a big girl. You know I always come to get you." But I didn't know it - I felt sad and forgotten.

Child Spirit

After that, I believed that I didn't matter, that I wasn't lovable, that the people I depended upon might not show up and I'd be all alone. I felt sad and scared and a little ashamed, because I didn't know yet how to be a *big girl*. I still wanted my mother.

In first grade, I fell in love with a little boy named Randy. Randy had polio and wore braces on his legs. He had one shoe that had a sole three inches thicker than the other. People in class made fun of me because he was my friend. I began to think, in my six-year-old mind, that it wasn't okay to be different or to have something wrong with you.

The next year when we were hiking a mountain with one of our family friends, I ran down a hill to get to one of my sisters who was lodged on the side of a cliff. The hill was so steep that I lost my balance and tumbled uncontrollably to the bottom. I was so banged up that the man who had taken us had to carry me out. I couldn't lift myself out of bed the next morning because my shoulder hurt so badly.

Mom wanted me to go to school with my arm in a sling, but I refused because I didn't want anyone to know something was wrong with me. My sisters chided, "You should have known better than to run down that hill," so again I believed I was stupid and wrong. All this by age eight.

But I kept my pride intact. I wouldn't let anyone know I was hurt. At school, I tried to swing and play on the merry-go-round. Sometimes the pain was excruciating but I was determined to be normal at all cost. Already the soul loss had begun.

A year or so later I was sitting on the couch in a sleeveless undershirt and Mom noticed that the right side of my collarbone looked disconnected. Apparently, I'd broken my collarbone the day I fell down the hillside. We hadn't really known because

I was never taken to the doctor. With no health insurance and such a big family, we had to be tough to survive.

By the end of second grade I had gone from being determined to be me to feeling that I must be a bad person. From then on I always felt a bit sad, depressed even, sometimes crying in front of the bathroom mirror because I didn't believe it was okay to feel. I needed to be a big girl. At least that was what I told myself. From those events, I crafted a story about who I was and I began to live in that story.

Sometimes I would feel utterly alone even though I had so many brothers and sisters. I'd sit on a grassy knoll along our driveway, string daisy necklaces together, and imagine that I was Cinderella. I couldn't understand why others didn't see that I was a precious little princess, and I dreamed of the prince who would someday discover and acknowledge the *real me*.

The Middle Years

My second-grade report card reads: "Colleen has read more books than anyone in the class." I loved learning. In the fifth grade, while the other girls were reading Nancy Drew mystery stories, I was reading autobiographies of Abigail Adams, Benjamin Franklin, Clara Barton, and many others. I was inspired by their courage and bravery.

In seventh grade, I went to see Sen. Robert F. Kennedy who was campaigning for the Presidency nearby. He spoke to a group of people from the back of a flatbed truck. My girlfriend and I stood on the steps going up to the cab and were within arm's length of the senator.

I remember being touched by the aura that emanated from him. He was pleasant and loving. And he was passionate that the world needed to change. Something in me caught fire that day. I began to believe, along with him, that humanitarian efforts were important. For years after, I collected articles on the Kennedys and kept them in a scrapbook.

During those years, many monumental changes occurred in history. I remember Dad calling us in one evening to watch the first man land on the moon. The nightly news was filled with bloody updates on the Vietnam War, riots at Kent state, and the assassinations of John F. Kennedy, Robert F. Kennedy, and Martin Luther King. Women's liberation began to have a voice. The world was astir and so was I.

Not only did I experience the normal angst and confusion that accompanies adolescence, I was also impacted and influenced by the collective turmoil and confusion around me. All the external authorities and institutions were called into question. Religions were dying, families were falling apart, education and corporations were all scrutinized. The youth of America were rising, the moral fiber of the country was challenged, and there were no mentors to lead the youth as the traditional structures crumbled. People questioned, "Is God dead?" But I was too young to understand how these events impacted my life or the decisions I made as I came of age.

Becoming a Woman

I reached puberty in the late '60s in the height of the sexual revolution. Like so many other kids, I received my sex education at school. During fifth grade, we girls were all called into a classroom for a special meeting and shown a movie about the changes our bodies (both boys and girls) would soon be going through. We were nervous and uncomfortable.

They gave us a beautiful pink pamphlet that we were supposed to share with our mothers. But I don't think any of us did. When I was younger, I remember Mom brought home a beautiful purple box of Kotex napkins and put it in her closet. Whenever I'd ask, "Mom, when are you going to let us use those nice napkins on the table?" She'd reply, "Someday!"

But she never once talked about menstruation to any of her seven daughters. I guess we were supposed to learn it at school. So, when all the other girls started wearing bras, I didn't feel I could ask my mother for a bra. Instead I saved my babysitting money until I had enough to buy one at the local shop. The shop owner helped me pick out my first bra and I wore it until it turned brown because I couldn't possibly throw it in the wash for Mom to see! Like she didn't know, right?

Growing Up

In the 6th grade, a cute Italian girl moved to our town from a hip town in California. She and I rode the school bus together, and she gave me the rest of my sex education by telling me what a *69* was and sharing about her first sexual encounters. I pretended that I understood, but I really didn't have a clue what she was talking about.

In the summer after 8th grade, I started my period. I was visiting some new friends in the state of Washington and, while there, my Aunt Mary drove us to a nearby town to go shopping. It was a hot summer day so I wore light-yellow shorts and a tee shirt. When we arrived at the store, it was obvious from my bloodstained shorts that I had started my period. Aunt Mary bought me the feminine supplies and a new pair of shorts so I could go out in public. She later made a phone call to my mother, saying (with a smile and a wink), "Well, your little *Colleenie* has become a woman today."

When we returned from shopping, my friend's brother noticed I was wearing a different pair of shorts and kept hounding me. "Where are your other shorts?" he asked with a knowing smirk. That was my initiation into womanhood and for some reason I felt sadder and more frightened than I could have anticipated. I was so homesick I had to call my mom, but of course we didn't talk about it.

When I returned home, Mom didn't say a word about my period and neither did I. I learned about tampons and the rest of the things I needed to know from my girlfriends.

Those years brought many changes to our family as well. Between my 7th and 8th grades my dad was elected city manager of our small town, which required that we sell our little *nature sanctuary* and move into town. My brother (the oldest in our family) was drafted and sent to Vietnam. My oldest sister got pregnant and had to get married.

My mother decided she wouldn't let the rest of her daughters date after that; it was how she would keep us from getting pregnant. One day I got in trouble for holding hands with a boy at school, but there was never an explanation as to why.

Mom just couldn't broach the subject of sex, so she became very rigid about it. Once, Dad wanted us to see our cow give birth, but Mom thought we were too young. She scolded my dad for suggesting such a thing.

Encounters with the Patriarchy

How might your life have been different if there had been a place for you? A place to go...a place of women, to help you to learn the ways of woman...a place where you were nurtured from an ancient flow sustaining you and steadying you as you sought to become yourself. A place of women to help you find and trust the ancient flow already there within yourself...waiting to be released...How might your life be different?

~ Judith Duerk, *Circle of Stones: Woman's Journey to Herself*

When I became sexually active at age 16 (it was, after all, the '60s), a friend of mine suggested that it would be smart to get on birth control pills. I agreed. So, we skipped school one day and went to a free clinic in a nearby town.

I was so nervous I could barely relax during the pelvic exam, because in spreading my legs I was betraying everything I had been taught by my parents and the Catholic Church. The male doctor doing the exam seemed restless and impatient, and his probing hands and tools were less than gentle. But I was determined to be responsible which was possible only because oral contraceptives were recently available.

A couple of weeks later I got called into the principal's office. He said, "I already talked to your friend and I know that you skipped school to get on birth control pills. I want you to know that you don't have to go around with a mattress strapped to your back to be liked. If you don't want me to tell your parents, you'll need to turn in all of your pills to me." No, not my parents! How could I face them about this? No...I mean yes...he was right. Perhaps I had been acting immorally and I needed to do the right thing. My parents couldn't know, that was a given. So, I gave my word and brought the pills to his office the next day. That was the end of the conversation.

Party Girl

But it didn't stop me from partying or being sexually active. It only made me feel more disconnected and less trusting of myself and of all the adults around me. Drinking made it easy not to think. Little did I know I was on a course headed for disaster.

At the beginning of my senior year I got pregnant and wasn't sure who the father was. Now I had something much worse to tell my parents.

I had to tell Mom because one day I was throwing up so much that she got worried I was becoming dehydrated. She suggested that I go to the doctor. "Could you possibly be pregnant?" asked the doctor. *No...no...NO! This cannot be happening. No!* I was a cheerleader, in my last year of school. Please, *God, no—not now!* But the test confirmed it was true.

Young, unmarried, and pregnant. It used to be the greatest shame that could befall a girl. ~ More Magazine

When I returned home to tell my mom, she cried. I had never before seen my mother cry because she said she'd lost her tears. I suppose, looking back, she was crying for me as much as for herself. She knew what having children meant.

"It's all my fault," she cried. But I knew it wasn't. She hadn't been there. She hadn't done the act. Her only fault was that she had been unavailable and rigid in her beliefs in a world that was rapidly changing. By her silence, she had forfeited her role as a trusted guide.

It was right after Thanksgiving when I found out I was pregnant. "Let's not tell your dad until after the holidays," Mom said. I hated that I had to keep this secret and that my life choices would impact everyone. I felt so ashamed.

One day I talked to her about the possibility of getting an abortion, even though they were still illegal. We both knew that having a child as an unwed

Fall from Grace

At that point, I felt more ashamed and afraid than ever. I hated the Catholic Church, my principal, and now the priest for telling me what to do with my life yet offering no guidance or support. *Yes, have the child! What you do from there is none of our business and certainly not our responsibility!* No wonder so many institutions were being overturned. They were impotent and out of touch with what was happening in the world. My helplessness turned into an inner rage directed at the Patriarchy.

One day my typing teacher wanted to know why I kept running to the bathroom during typing class. I told him the news. His face turned pale. He said, "I'll have to tell the principal."

Ironically the principal never said another word to me. But unlike the other girls who had gotten pregnant, I was never asked to leave school.

Many people have set their own intuitive guidance aside, replacing it with the opinions of parents, teachers, experts, or leaders in a variety of disciplines. But the more you look to others for their guidance, the more removed you become from your own wise counsel.

~ Esther Hicks, *The Law of Attraction*

Wearing the Scarlet Letter

My mother made me stay home from school on Fridays after she found out I was pregnant. I was a cheerleader and she didn't think I should be in a leadership role in my condition. Of course, that was another loss for me and a nail in my coffin of shame.

One Friday after the new year, I received a call from my girlfriend. "Everyone knows! Everyone is whispering at their lockers, asking me if it's true. What should I say?" It was the kind of gossip that thrives in a small town.

mother would change everything. So instead of saying, "No, absolutely not!" she suggested I make an appointment to talk with the young priest in the next town. I'm sure she knew that he would never condone an abortion, because the Catholic Church didn't even allow birth control (thus, my mother and her nine children).

I went hoping for something—guidance, perhaps - I wasn't really sure. As I sat across the desk from him, the handsome priest listened. He was very quiet. Then he said, "I cannot give you permission to have an abortion." And that was it: no counsel, no emotional support, and no Come-to-Jesus talk. Nothing. He might as well have said, "You're on your own, kid," because that's exactly how I felt.

My worst nightmare was about to begin. I hung up the phone in tears and, at that moment, Dad came in for his morning tea break. There was no escaping it now. He had to be told.

We gathered around the oak kitchen table that had once been his mother's, I sat with my eyes downcast, tears streaming down my face. "What's wrong?" he asked as he looked from me to my mother.

"Everyone knows," she said. She had already told him I was pregnant, but they'd never once said a word to me. He slowly lifted his cup, took a sip of tea, looked out into space for a moment and then said, "Everyone makes mistakes. You just happened to make one that is going to show." I wonder if he meant to say, "You just happened to make one that is going to change the course of your life forever."

That comment was the only one my father ever made to me about my pregnancy. It was clear that he was not going to reject me or send me to a home for unwed mothers, which was one of the options I had considered for myself. He loved me for who I was, but I was so ashamed I could not accept it.

A Girl without a Dream

Other than moving out of my parents' house when I turned 18, I had no dreams. I hadn't been taught to dream. I had been taught to find a job with the thought that it would take me where I needed to go. I hadn't a clue what I was supposed to do with my life.

Once I asked my mom, "How come I don't have any talents?" She replied, "You have so many, they're hard to name." She never mirrored back to me what I was good at. It seemed obvious when I looked at my sisters - they could knit, crochet, cook. But my talents seemed elusive.

As a young girl, I wanted to join Girl Scouts or ballet, but with limited finances and a large family to care for, my parents never supported these *wants*. In the third grade, we were so poor that my mom didn't have a dollar to give me to buy the flutophone and

booklet I needed to be able to practice with the rest of the students. Instead, the teacher had a flutophone that she let me use during class. It was a black one, unlike the white flutophones all the other kids had. So, I couldn't practice at home, and when it came time for our performance the only thing I could do was blow the tune into the flutophone itself. As I stood in front of the audience I felt embarrassed and ashamed.

After taking my SATs in high school, my Algebra and Geometry teacher called my mother and me in for a conference to inform us that I had scored high on the test, and that my mother should try to get me into college. That meant nothing to me at the time and perhaps not so much to my mother, either, since she didn't have the means to send me to college anyway.

In June of 1973 and seven months pregnant, I marched with the rest of my peers in our graduation ceremony. My path was laid out before me. I would be a mother in a couple of months and would not only need to learn how to take care of myself, but how to take care of my child as well. I gave birth to my son on August 2, 1973, I named him Matthew, because it meant *a gift from God*. I knew that to be true even though I didn't know how or why. As I launched into my new life as a young adult and single-mother, I didn't know he would be the catalyst for me to step into my highest potential and most empowered self.

Opportunities to find deeper powers in ourselves come when life seems most challenging.

~ Joseph Campbell

Leap and the Bridge Will Appear

Back in the '70s, the work world didn't look upon single moms as good candidates for jobs. Maybe they judged them as losers or irresponsible. The opposite was true, at least for me though: when you're hungry, you show up for work.

Leaving Home

I was scared. Who did I think I was anyway? No one in my family had ever earned a college degree. When I received my first biology test results, my worst fears were confirmed: *I didn't have what it took to succeed in college.* Scribbled across the top of the page was a big, fat, red F.

I tried to breathe and choke back the tears, but I couldn't. I was devastated. Why did I think that I could pull this off? What was I thinking? I gave it my best and I failed.

> *Hardships often prepare ordinary people for an extraordinary destiny.*
>
> ~C.S. Lewis

Fortunately, the teacher noticed my distress. He came up to me after class and said, "Let's talk."

He asked me many questions, found out a little bit about my story and then said, "It sounds like you've been out of school long enough that you've forgotten how to study. I think you can do this. What I'd like to do is set you up with another student as a study partner to see if we can improve your grade."

In a few days, he introduced me to a cute guy who was my teacher's most enthusiastic student. He was smart and willing to work with me. With his help, I was able to manifest a B in biology.

The teacher became my friend and over the Thanksgiving holiday, he invited my son and me to dinner. He continued to encourage me to believe in myself. He helped me not just with his class but all the way through two years at the community college and into a four-year university

He showed up in my life at the right moment, a moment when I might have given up had I been left alone with my own self-talk. For that reason, I am eternally grateful for him. That experience confirmed the premise that when the hero or heroine is ready, the teachers show up.

I was fortunate to find a woman who was willing to give me a chance to work as a receptionist for an insurance company. In the beginning, it was a good job. It gave me the opportunity to get some work experience, prove myself, and it provided me a community. Two other women about my age worked there and we quickly became friends. They didn't seem to care that I was a single mom.

Four years later, struggling to make ends meet, I realized that I would never overcome poverty by working at that job so I needed to get an education. I gave up my full-time position, took two part-time jobs working for agents, received enough grant and loan money for one term, took the leap, and started college.

Battling Depression

Before my last term of college, I signed up for 16 credits and started a full-time job in a town an hour away. I realized that once I graduated I would have no money; I would have student loans to repay in addition to all my other living expenses. Each morning I sent my son to school, worked a full day, and then commuted home at night to study.

I'm not sure how I managed to reach graduation day, but I did. By that time, I was exhausted. My parents came up and took my son to the ceremony. When I received my diploma, he cried, but my parents sat there stoically. Afterwards they took my son, my sister and me out to lunch. I felt sad because it hardly seemed to be a celebration of me. It was heartbreaking for me to receive such little acknowledgment after all my hard work. But my mom always said it was difficult to celebrate any one of her children because doing so would make the others feel bad.

The day after graduation, my son and I moved so I wouldn't have to commute to work. Just like that ... I was into my new life. I was still broke, but at least I was working in advertising (which is what I had studied) and I was hopeful that something would change.

The town we moved to was not really where I wanted to live. It was small town, conservative America at its best, with the unflattering nickname of *armpit of Oregon*. The biggest employer in town was a toxic paper mill which, quite frankly, made the area stink. I had hoped for something more romantic for my life. Instead of feeling happy about my accomplishments, I felt sad and disillusioned. Had I worked this hard just to get *here*? No one had warned me that life transitions could be so difficult.

We were even poorer now with my school loans to repay. I had a couch propped up with cinder blocks and a fireplace, but no wood. How depressing! Some days I found myself sitting at my desk at work, barely

Endings

holding back the tears. I searched *help wanted* ads and discovered a weekly newspaper in Portland, Oregon that was looking for an advertising sales representative. I applied and got the job. A new job in Portland - now that was more like the vision I had for my life! I even had sisters who lived there so I would not be alone. I was both excited and scared.

Expansion

My sister, who was recently divorced with four kids of her own, let me move in with her until I could get established in my job. She'd just given birth to twin girls. Her husband had left them when she was pregnant, so now she was a working single-mom, as well. Perhaps we could help each other. By this time, the early '80s, single-parent families were becoming the *norm*.

The first couple of weeks were chaotic. I'd never lived in Portland and my job required that I go downtown to call on shop owners to advertise in our publication. I drove over the freeway bridges with no clue which off ramps to take. Of course, this was before Map Quest and GPS devices.

To make matters worse, my car broke down and my son's appendix ruptured. I was grateful for a lady at work who offered to let me drive her little sports car. In my small-town naiveté, I thought she was just being nice; I didn't realize until later that she had a crush on me.

The sights and sounds of the city were new to me. As I wandered the downtown area, calling on businesses, I saw a whole new world. I discovered shops I never knew existed; ways to make a living I'd never considered. I felt alive for the first time in a long time.

I joined a sales forum and connected with a tribe of *metaphysical people* who were into personal, spiritual, and financial growth and expansion. At my job, we had to read Dale Carnegie's book, How to Win Friends and Influence People. These ideas began to take seed and grow in me; I started to see what was possible for my future. My *inner dreamer* awakened.

Through work I met a couple who wanted to advertise in our publication. They were life coaches and sold Paul J. Meyer's Dynamics of Personal Goal Setting course. The program cost $500. They promised me that if I met with them on a weekly basis and did the required work, it would change my life. I didn't have $500, but I had a credit card with that much credit. I decided to take the risk.

In working the program, I learned not only how to dream but how to put a foundation under my dreams. I learned how to set goals and to make commitments. I learned how to create affirmations and to change my negative fears and beliefs.

Within a few years of working with them, I would have a job that would allow me to achieve my income goal and have a home and car ...everything I had dreamed of.

> *Crystallize your goals. Make a plan for achieving them and set yourself a deadline. Then, with supreme confidence, determination, and disregard for obstacles and other people's criticisms, carry out your plan.*
>
> ~ Paul J. Meyer

Iguana Love You Like No One Has Before-The Turning Point

One of my big dreams was to get married. At 29 years of age, I had been a single-mom for 12 years and was weary from doing everything myself. Marriage and partnership seemed like the next right step.

Dennis and I met at a wedding and were immediately smitten. He was 12 years older than me and was not scared that I had a child because he had been married and divorced, and had two nearly-grown kids of his own.

He was charming, romantic, financially secure, and drove a BMW—all attractive traits to a young woman who dreamed of a better life. When he noticed my car had bald tires, he bought me new ones. When he noticed I had only a light-weight coat, he bought me a heavier one. Finally, a man who was willing to take care of us!

It seemed like a no-brainer when he asked me a few months later to move in with him. I was still living with my sister and her four kids and was barely making ends meet. Here was the possibility of a life I'd only imagined.

The day I moved in with him, Dennis handed me a card with a heart and a cute picture of an Iguana on it that read: *Iguana love you like no one has before.* At last, here was my knight in shining armor! I felt a bit like Julia Roberts in the movie *Pretty Woman*.

Our romance lasted a short while before the realities of blending families started to creep in and the limitations of past wounds started to make themselves known. I had been so rejected in my teen years that I had no idea how to open my heart and love someone.

We married within a year of meeting one another; soon after, Dennis' teen daughter moved in with us. We now had two kids who had to adjust to new people in their lives. My son, who previously had my undivided attention, felt a little disappointed. He had dreamed of a *Cosby dad* and instead got a human one who made rules and was sometimes critical and short-tempered. Dennis' daughter was sure I was going to hurt her dad and steal his love from her.

It became evident after a while that we had both entered the marriage a little naively and with some unrealistic expectations. We also each carried our own wounds around love and our fears that we might be either unlovable or that there would not be

In Relationship

enough love to go around. Our honeymoon period was short-lived as the tensions of *real life* emerged.

The good news is that it got me into counseling to explore the wounds of my childhood and the abandonment issues I carried with me. At first, I went to counseling by myself. What is memorable about the experience is that I worked with a woman, a *mother figure* who told me that I could trust myself. That was a big turning point because, up until then, I had looked outward for answers since my mom had been so controlling.

Later, Dennis and I went to my counselor as a couple; we took a Myers-Briggs personality test to help reveal the differences and strengths we each brought

23

to our marriage. She taught us not to consider each other wrong for our differing perspectives on the world (his being left-brained and mine, primarily right-brained), but to appreciate and work with those differences. She also taught us that because of our differences we looked for love in different ways; we needed to show our love to the other person in the way he/she could receive it.

Good relationships don't just happen. They take time, patience and two people who truly want to be together.

~ Author Unknown

I also signed up for a three-month co-dependency class and I became conscious of the patterns I had carried forth from childhood. At that time, I had a low self-esteem and I carried a story within me that I was a victim. The facilitator helped me see how dysfunctional it was to carry a victim mentality and she challenged me to let go of that image so that I could become more empowered.

My marriage and new family dynamics provided fertile ground for me to see everything that was unhealed and just how lost I had become. I felt a mess much of the time, as the emotions I had stuffed down over the years bubbled to the surface.

It didn't help that Dennis' temperament was similar to my father's. On one hand, he was deeply compassionate and loving; on the other, angry and critical. I never knew which behavior would surface when.

Whenever Dennis became angry with me, my feelings were hurt and I was like a three-year-old with no adult resources available to address the problems between us. All I could do was cry which, I'm sure, angered him even more.

One day he said, "You're going to have to learn how to stand up to me or I'm going to run over the top of you." So, I did. With time, I learned to find my voice, speak up and defend myself, rather than collapse—

which had been my main coping skill up until then. This helped to equalize our relationship.

Character cannot be developed in ease and quiet. Only through experiences of trial and suffering can the soul be strengthened, vision cleared, ambition inspired and success achieved. ~ Helen Keller

Early in our marriage we sold the house in the city and moved to a house overlooking the Sandy River, near Mt. Hood. There we created a home for our kids that was connected to nature. Although our lives were at times tumultuous, there was love and the fate that brought us all together.

The illusion I had held, that marriage meant *happily ever after*, collapsed. There was no *knight in shining armor*, no *Cosby dad*, just people doing the best they could with the skills they had. At 30 years of age, it was time for me to grow up. Thus began my search for healing and wholeness.

Becoming the Father of My Own Experience

One of the other dreams I had (in addition to getting married) was to increase my earnings from $25,000 to $50,000 a year. I was tired of living in poverty. I had worked hard to change my life and I was determined to succeed.

Shortly after we met, Dennis helped me get an interview as a sales representative for the Yellow Pages. It had a small base pay, but a good possibility for increased income through their commission system. After three interviews, I was hired.

The first year it seemed that nearly everyone I called on wanted to cancel their advertising, claiming that it hadn't worked. The way the union contract read, I got debited for a percentage of every sales dollar lost, so I often ended the day in debt. Such a discouraging system, especially since I was new on the job and just learning what the product could do.

Management posted employees' names and performances on a chart every day. For a long time, my name was at the bottom of the list and many nights I'd go home crying from the stress and pressure from my job. I was being tested again, it seemed! Did I have what it took to create my dreams? The only reason I stayed in that job was that I knew the union contract would soon be renegotiated and the debit system was one of the things being challenged. So, I stuck it out, did my affirmations, and kept believing that it would get better, even when I didn't know how it would improve.

When the union contract was renewed, my base salary doubled, things began to level out and, eventually my income rose. A year later I received the Circle of Excellence Award and an all-expense-paid trip to Disney World for being one of the top performers for the year.

Working Girl

I was still unhappy. The *ram 'em and jam 'em* attitude that came with the job was contrary to everything I believed. The price of success was high.

When I reached my income goal, I realized that I made more money in one year than my father had ever made. It was one of those threshold moments. What if my father was no longer the supreme authority in my life? What role would he play in my life now that I was his financial equal or superior? Would it change how we saw one another? I had finally reached the financial independence that women of previous generations had fought for, but I still felt incomplete and disillusioned.

On one hand, I felt empowered that I could set a goal and, with intention and persistence, achieve it. I had become the father of my own experience. I had made it in the masculine world.

But on the other hand, instead of coasting into satisfied bliss, my soul clamored for more. Something was missing. I had achieved success in the outer world, but there as an unfulfilled longing inside me. In my journals I described it as a *longing to blossom*. Something more yearned to be expressed through me.

I sometimes went with a friend to listen to a man who channeled spiritual energies. He explained that what I was feeling was a longing to awaken spiritually. He validated my angst. In response, I meditated, worked in my journal, and prayed for a way to relieve myself of my chronic dissatisfaction with life.

Signs of Change

In the fall of 1990, the carefully constructed life I had built and fought for began to unravel. I found out that my sister's new husband (the sister I had lived with earlier) had sexually molested several of her daughters. My other two sisters and I did our best to emotionally support them, but we all started to feel traumatized, as if we had been sexually abused before. Even though none of us could recall any specific event, we were all shaken to the core.

It prompted me to work with a counselor again, because I couldn't quite shake the depression I felt. My first visit to the new counselor included taking an assessment test. On the second visit, she reported that my test came back showing I was, indeed, suffering from depression, so I made another appointment to see her after the first of the year.

Around this same time, I had a profound dream that I was watching an Indian village burn. Inside one of the tipis was a badly-burned little girl, screaming to be rescued. From my vantage point in the dream, I didn't know if it would be more humane to let her die or attempt to rescue her, since she would be scarred for life. But I pulled her out

of the flames and then awoke. Somehow, I sensed intuitively that she was a younger version of me. I needed to rescue myself, and if the dream was any indication, there was a long road to healing.

Shortly before the holidays I left my wallet in a shopping cart in a parking lot and by the time I called the store to see if they had found it, someone had already taken it and used my credit card. I had to report the theft to all the credit card companies and obtain a new driver's license. This seemed metaphorical: I recognized that, on some level, it was time for a new identity.

Shape of Things to Come

Amid the chaos, Dennis and I were preparing to visit family in Bend, Oregon, over the holidays and then travel to Pasadena for the Rose Bowl. We'd both been working hard on our jobs and were looking forward to some much-needed fun and relaxation.

As part of my work, I had been reading books on prosperity and spending time doing visualizations and affirmations. A few days before we left, I went into our bedroom where Dennis was resting on the bed and said, "I don't know why, but I can FEEL that prosperity is going to come. I know it's coming!" He rolled his eyes and smiled. I'm sure he was thinking, *"There she goes again!"* But I couldn't shake this deep knowing that my life was about ready to change in ways both positive and profound.

Gathering Your Story Elements

Stories help us discover who we are. They are what make us unique. Where we lived; our family of origin, economic background, and religious/spiritual influences; and the political and social climate all affected our lives in some way. They shaped who we have become.

The Storyteller

Discover how these elements have impacted your life.

Exercise 1 - Free Association

Supplies:

o   journal   o   pen

Label a page in your journal for each of the following topics (allow at least 3-4 pages for each one):

- story characters
- places
- geographical landscape
- economics
- religion/faith
- social/political environment
- stories your family told about you
- early traumas/wounds

Explore each topic and jot down whatever associations come to mind. Feel free to return to this exercise when you feel called to add more information.

View your life as if it were a fairy tale. What is the landscape? Where did you lose touch with your true self? Who were the villains, the teachers? What were the turning points that set you on your journey to wholeness? What were the wounds, the traumas, and false beliefs you need to overcome?

Exercise 2 - Artful Play

Supplies:

- couple sheets of blank paper
- pen
- scissors
- colorful markers
- assorted papers
- glue stick
- paper doll template

If you played with paper dolls as a child, you know how much fun they can be! In this exercise we're going to make connecting paper dolls to represent some of your story characters. Download the template from my website (see page 6 for details).

Print a couple copies of the template on blank paper and cut them out. Next, feel free to decorate them by adding hair, facial features, clothing, shoes... use your markers (or anything that makes them come alive for you). Or you can cut out special papers for hair and clothing and glue them on as I have done here. The invitation is to have fun!

When you're done, cut the dolls apart and glue each one onto a separate page in your journal. Then, identify each character and write down as many of their qualities that come to mind. Try to recognize the humanness of each of your characters and imagine how their story elements might have shaped them and, in turn, may have shaped you. Make any additional notes in your journal that may have surfaced for you.

Exercise 3 - Photographs

If you have photographs of your family of origin, take an afternoon and go through them. Photocopy the pictures that are of particular interest and insert them into your journal. Notice what you notice. Make notes. It doesn't matter if you left enough blank pages behind each category or if what you create is not perfect. (Remember we're seeking wholeness, not perfection.) See the images as clues and doorways to understanding the places and experiences that helped shape you.

29

Winter's Glow

The Unraveling

For a seed to achieve its greatest expression, it must come completely undone. The shell cracks, its insides come out and everything changes. To someone who doesn't understand growth, it would look like complete destruction.
~ Cynthia Occelli

On Christmas Eve in 1990, Dennis, Matthew, and I crawled out of bed before daybreak to begin our vacation. We were excited! As soon as we arrived in Bend, we stopped by my sister's house (where we were to celebrate the holiday) to pick up my brother-in-law and nephew for a day of skiing on Mt. Bachelor.

We were elated when we reached the mountain to find sun and near spring-like conditions, especially since we'd been socked in with fog for days on end in Portland. It couldn't have been a more perfect day.

On our last run before lunch, Dennis stopped and doubled over in pain. He assured me and my brother-in-law that he would be fine. "I just need to get off the mountain and sit down," he said. But I could feel my alarms going off. Was he having a heart attack? Would I have to give him CPR...Would I know how, especially up here on the side of a ski slope? He must have noticed my concern because he said, "I'm okay. I must be getting the flu or something. I just need to get off the mountain and get something to drink."

When we arrived at the lodge, Dennis again reassured me that he would be fine. I went into the lodge to get him a Coke. I returned, handed it to him and he said, "I think this might be more serious. Go in and have the lady at the desk call 911. I think I might be having a heart attack."

"Oh, God!" I ran back into the lodge. The lady at the booth was on the phone. I yelled to her, "Call 911, I think my husband is having a heart attack!" About that same time, I heard someone from outside yell, "There's a man down on the deck!" I knew it was Dennis.

I ran outside to find Dennis flat on his back, eyes rolling back into his head. I knelt to unzip his bibs and a man pushed me aside; he said he was a doctor. My brother-in-law and I stood nearby in shock and disbelief, yelling at Dennis to please come back. "Fight it, come back...COME BACK...please, come back! Please!"

The man performed CPR for what seemed like a long time, but there was no response. We all watched helplessly. How could this be happening? It felt so surreal and yet real at the same time.

Then a man from the ski patrol wrapped his arms around me from behind, reassuring me that everything that could be done was being done. The Life Flight helicopter had been called and was on its way, but it would still be several minutes before it arrived. I could feel him pull me away from the scene. He suggested I go into the ski patrol room and wait for the helicopter, so I would be warm. "But I want to go with Dennis when the helicopter arrives." He assured me I would be informed when it was time.

Meanwhile, the ski patrol had the boys gather our gear and load it into the car. By the time I was led back outside, the sound of the rotor blades was echoing off the outer walls of the building as the helicopter ascended into the air. I watched as it disappeared. Why had it left without me?

On the car ride down the mountain, I tried to come to grips with the idea that Dennis was most likely dead; but my son kept insisting he had watched them try to revive Dennis with the shock paddles and it had worked. "He's alive, Mom! I know he's alive!" I knew better. I had seen Dennis leave his body and it had been too long with no response for him to be alive. Perhaps Matthew had seen something I hadn't; I wanted desperately to hold on to that glimmer of hope.

When we walked into the emergency room, a doctor led me into a small room that seemed no bigger than a closet. "Have a seat." he said. "I'm sorry to tell you that your husband is dead. He did not make it." My head began to spin. I quickly excused myself and ran into the bathroom to vomit. When I returned, a nurse was standing by the door. She led me into a bigger room across the hall and sat me at an empty table and handed me a phone. "You need to call his family," she said. "You'll need their support to get through this. It's not going to get any easier."

I dialed his parents' number. "Hello. Hi, Marv, I'm calling from the hospital to let you know that Dennis died today." I sat there stunned as I listened to him gasp.

"Where do you want his body taken?" asked the nurse. "By law, we can only keep him here for a few hours." I wanted to scream. "I don't want his body taken anywhere! I just want my husband back and this nightmare to end!" But decisions had to be made.

When we returned to my sister's house, more of my family had gathered to celebrate the Christmas Eve festivities. They were shocked and speechless, nervous about how to respond. The smell of roasted turkey filled the air.

"Do we have dinner and open the presents...or what?" asked my eldest sister.

We decided that it would be better to carry on because the children still needed to have a Christmas. The flow of life hadn't stopped because Dennis had died. I sat numbly on the couch, eyes glazed with shock, while they went through the motions of Christmas. My husband, at 47, was dead... and I was a widow at 35. It *wasn't supposed to happen this way.*

That night when I went to bed, I searched through the brown paper bag the hospital had given me with Dennis' belongings. I opened his wallet and rummaged through his ID and credit cards, hoping to find a clue as to where he had gone. I counted his money. His keys lay on the dresser. *How could this be?*

Sitting in the Ashes

After the holidays, I returned to my sales job. People either avoided me or wrapped their arms around me in disbelief. I knew I was not the same person who had left for the holidays. I felt a little like Humpty Dumpty who had a great fall. The past was gone, wiped out. I had no idea if life would ever come back together again or what it would look like if it did.

I can't even begin to express what a godsend it was to already have had a counseling appointment set up. When I met with the counselor to work on my depression, she asked, "How were your holidays?"

"My husband died on Christmas Eve," I said. After a long pause, we began what would become a year-and-a-half long journey through my depression and grief. She became my trusted guide; I, the willing student.

Each week I made my way to the counselor's office to release the feelings raging inside me. I felt so lost, confused, lonely, and scared—overwhelmed by the feelings and responsibilities that were once again upon my shoulders.

At the same time, life insurance checks began to arrive in my mail box. Ironically, Dennis' death meant I would have financial freedom for the first time in my life. The money had come. I could decide now what I wanted to do with my life. But my life and psyche were in such disarray that I hadn't a clue what I wanted. I had no dreams. They lay in ashes at my feet. Receiving financial security in this way was

Broken Hearted

bittersweet. I would have traded it all to have my husband and my old life back. But that was not an option and I felt grateful for the support. It too was a godsend.

The Long Road to Healing

Your most profound and intimate experiences of worship will likely be in your darkest days—when your heart is broken, when you feel abandoned, when you're out of options, when the pain is great—and you turn to God alone. ~ Rick Warren, *The Purpose Driven Life*

In early February, my son informed me that he could graduate from high school early. He had plenty of credits and wanted to be free to pursue his dream of becoming a professional snowboarder. I'm sure he also wanted to escape the all-consuming grief which engulfed our home. Again, my heart wrenched. *Not this too!*

"You need to let your son go," my counselor advised. "He needs to take his own journey. It will not help either of you to have him be your surrogate husband."

I trusted her guidance but it felt like another big loss, another part of my life being stripped away. It only compounded my grief. I was angry with God and Dennis for leaving. This wasn't the way my life was supposed to unfold!

Instinctively I knew I had to be open to the pain in order to heal. Some days the intensity of the grief dropped me to my knees and darkness smothered me. My counselor reminded me that I could trust the grief to take me where I needed to go. But there were days when I felt as though it would never end,

and that it would be easier to let my car roll into an on-coming truck just to end my misery.

I willed myself back into life, but everything I tried fell flat. I changed positions in the company to lessen my stress, but it only added more. I wanted to build a home as a way of building a new dream for myself, but I couldn't seem to muster the strength to create it. The *doing* part of myself was no longer in charge. I was at the mercy of some unknown force...and I was angry!

Meeting the Ski Patrol Man

The support of others was palpable, but it was a mixed blessing. Some people just didn't know

Inner Wisdom

34

what to say or do, so they went out of their way to avoid me. Others felt obligated to tell me how the grieving process was *supposed* to unfold. They didn't understand that grief is organic and has little regard for any rule that may have been written. Yet I knew that people cared, and that I was loved.

At times, it was hard to let that love in since I'd never been taught how to receive it. But I was deeply grateful. I did my best to send notes to people who had supported me, including the staff at the Sunrise Lodge and the ski patrol man who had supported me that day.

I received a card from him. He shared how difficult it had been for him and the ski patrol team to witness the death of my husband. He had just gotten divorced and was going through his own cycle of loss and grief. I was touched by his compassion.

I wrote him back to offer my sympathy and thus began an on-going dialogue between the two of us. I told him that I would be going to Bend in the summer to leave some mementos and prayers on the mountain in honor of Dennis' passing. He wrote back to say that if I wanted to ride the ski lift to the top of the mountain, he could arrange it and he offered to accompany me if I wished. I agreed.

His support was helpful and meaningful. He was handsome, loving, gentle, and respectful. After the first year of grief, our mutual loss and respect for one another began to move more towards a relationship. It felt safe to explore, because he lived in Bend, and I in Portland. We continued to communicate through cards and phone calls. At age 36, I knew I was not ready to live alone for the rest of my days.

Eventually he and I saw each other about once a month. Many times, he came to Portland and we

went out to enjoy music or the arts. I suppose it was healing for both of us. We could explore a relationship without the expectation or pressure that it needed to go anywhere, because we both knew we were in a healing process.

It was helpful to share the unfolding relationship with my counselor and have her guidance, I learned how to build a healthy relationship.

Breakdown of the Body

Nine months into my grief, my body began to break down under the stress. One afternoon at work, I felt terribly ill. My back went into seizures. I managed to get myself home but the next day I had to ask my boss to take me to the doctor's office because I couldn't walk. I had to be wheeled into the office. I had never been so incapacitated and I was scared.

The doctor assumed my back had gone out, so he sent me home with pain pills. But the pain did not go away. I went to a massage therapist who was both a healer and a psychic. She said it didn't seem like it was my back. She was concerned about my condition. Later that day I started vomiting. I could not keep anything down. I developed such a high fever that the sheets were soaked. Every day after that I woke up thinking I would be better, but nothing changed. A concerned friend came and stayed with me for a couple of days. I got so weak that I started hallucinating. I could feel myself floating out of my body. I could see all kinds of art work. I thought I was dying, but I was too weak to care.

The massage therapist called to check on me. She said, "Your organs are shutting down. I will be right there! We need to get some fluids in you now!" She came to my house and gave me an enema and sat with me for hours, putting ice chips into my mouth. The next day I turned a corner and began to get well. I don't know what might have happened had she not called.

From that time on though, my body was never the same. I ached continually and went to chiropractors for relief, only to find none. Although I was never diagnosed, I believe I developed an auto-immune disease which lasted for the next 20 years.

I was better by the time my son returned from Europe. He said, "Oh, Mom, you've got to see the art I saw in Europe!" Amazing, I thought. His pictures looked like the art pieces I had seen during my illness.

The Call

I continued to work with my counselor, not only on my grief, but on understanding my co-dependency and family of origin issues. We left no stone unturned. One day I went to her convinced that I was going crazy because I couldn't stop crying. My body, mind, and spirit were exhausted. I had spent too many years efforting as a single mom and now grieving as a widow to continue to hold it together anymore.

She reassured me, "You are not going crazy, but I do think you should consider giving up your job. You're like a cup that is overflowing. You need to let go to make room for something new to emerge. I think it's time for you to find your true self," she said. I didn't know exactly what she meant, but I knew it resonated with me.

Instead of feeling elated, I felt even more sadness. I had not thought about the loss of community that would happen by giving up my job. Who was I if I was no longer a wife, a mother, an employee? What was the meaning of my life? Why did I exist? These were the questions I had to answer.

Emerging

Sometimes all you can do is bow your head and weather the storm.

~ Source Unknown

At some point, I realized I was on a much bigger journey than just getting through a year-long grief cycle. I was not only grieving the loss of my husband, my son, and my job; I was also grieving the death of my old self, the self I had once been. It was clear that I was no longer in control of my life.

Encounters with the Feminine

One day, my best friend invited me to a women's drumming circle. There I learned about the work of Judith Durek, who wrote, Circle of Stones, A Woman's Journey to Herself. In the opening lines of her book, she essentially posed the question: If our true-nature had been embraced and we were, indeed, nourished when we were discovering our true identity, how might our life have been different?

When I learned that Judith was offering a weekend retreat, I decided to attend. Her position was that many women had lost touch with themselves and did not trust their own wisdom and knowledge because they had grown up in a culture that did not honor the feminine. Durek believed women needed to descend into their depths to discover their true selves.

> *Women too have often colluded with the masculine, denied their own power and natural magic, and instead accepted masculine values and ways of thinking. They have betrayed their own deepest selves.*
>
> ~ Llewellyn Vaughan-Lee, *Reclaiming the Feminine Mystery of Creation*

Several women attended the retreat. The first night, we explored our feminine lineage and thought about who our female ancestors were, where they had come from, and how they had lived. We were invited to introduce ourselves as "daughter of Kathleen and granddaughter of Mary Kate Kelly," in honor of the women who had come before us.

The next day we began to descend into the depths of our souls. We'd built enough trust that the stories the women carried within them surfaced. Judith tenderly witnessed and mirrored back to each of us, as we shared our stories and pain with one another. There was one woman who went into a rage as she talked about the disconnect she felt with her family. She slammed her body against the wall and, at first, I was scared. I didn't know what to do; but Judith asked us to just stand, be present, and open our hearts with love as we witnessed her. I did as she instructed. When the woman was done raging, she turned around and looked at us. Judith asked, "What's different this time?" The woman replied, "You're all still here."

Witnessing that encounter gave me hope because I knew, on a visceral level, that the experience (being held and observed from a place of love) made it possible for the woman to create a new story. For the first time in my life I felt joy. I knew healing was possible for me, for all of us!

Taking Flight

After I quit my job, I set my son up in an apartment, put my belongings into storage, and planned a trip to Ireland, England, and Scotland. The gift of my loss of identity was that I was no longer attached to or responsible for anyone except myself. I was free at last to find me.

My travels began at the Findhorn Foundation—a spiritual community in Scotland known for their transformational, self-discovery work. I hadn't intended to go there, but when a mail strike prevented me from making the connections to a writing program at Trinity College in Dublin, my friend (the same one who had taken me to the drumming circles) suggested I might enjoy a visit there.

At Findhorn, I met people from all over Europe who were also searching for a deeper spiritual connection. Most all of them felt that the trappings of the outer world were no longer enough. Like me, they longed to connect to something that had more depth and meaning. I could see I was not alone in the journey and that the call I was feeling was also alive in them.

During the days, we meditated, shared in groups, learned dances of antiquity, worked in the gardens, and learned about the spirits of the earth. Overall it was an enriching experience that immediately connected me in an intimate way with others of like mind. We learned about the Goddess and the power of love. We got to see, just down the road from where we were staying, monuments where witches (women) had been burned for their beliefs and gifts. It made the history of the Goddess and the loss of the feminine a reality.

Next, I traveled to the island of Iona off the coast of Scotland, to attend a workshop, *Birthing the Undivided Self*, designed to help participants heal the divide between their inner and outer worlds. There, as the wind and rain whipped against the windows of our small cottage, I learned how to listen to the wisdom of my soul. I learned that the soul communicates through a symbolic language often using synchronicity, intuition, visions, dreams, and archetypes to communicate.

As we explored the life/death/rebirth cycle, I learned that God enters our hearts through the broken places. For the first time, I felt affirmed that my journey through grief had a much larger purpose. I was being emptied and hallowed so something new could emerge. I also learned that to connect to our soul requires stillness. Quite a contrast to the busy corporate world I had just left.

I met a friend who was visiting from Portland after the workshop was over and we spent several days touring England and Ireland. When she left, I stayed in Ireland with the elderly couple who owned my grandmother's land. Dennis and I had searched and found them years earlier, when we went to Ireland on our honeymoon. They had adopted me as their own.

The man was just a little boy when my grandmother left Ireland, but he remembered my great-grandmother and shared lots of stories with me about her and the place where she lived. He said that before the famine many had settled in the surrounding area. One day he took me hiking through the fields and up the hill to where my great-grandmother's cottage had once stood. All that remained was a pile of rocks covered with berry vines.

You can't know yourself if you don't know your history.
~ Clarissa Pinkola Estés

The history of my Irish ancestors came alive for me and I began to understand how their history influenced who I became. Their story and legacy was a part of me. My personal angst was not caused solely by my mother or father; it was the story of the life I inherited. Catholicism gave me a foundation of faith, and my Celtic roots provided a legacy, a story, of poverty and oppression, as well as, strength, respect for the land, and the full integration of faith in every-day life. I could forgive and let go.

After Ireland, I decided to return to the Island of Iona and spend a month writing about my experiences through grief. Some part of me had always longed to be a writer. Now, I felt I had something of value to share.

Grieving and Searching

I rented a cottage that sat in the middle of the pasture facing the sea. I was alone—alone with my thoughts, memories, a manual typewriter, and a coal burning fireplace. It was here that I wrote about what I had learned from my journey through grief.

Ironically, I still didn't know who I was. I only knew that I wanted to live with God at the center, to live a life that had heart and meaning. For now, I would write.

Each day I challenged myself to write for a couple of hours. Most days I sobbed my way through the pages as I relived my story. I learned that telling one's story is an important part of the healing process.

Eventually, isolation set in. With no TV or outer distractions, the hours seemed endless. I felt homesick. The island was so small that it took less than an hour to walk the length of it. Many days the ocean storms made it difficult to get outside. It also meant that the mail, which was my life-line, would not come ashore.

The woman who rented the cottage to me sensed my homesickness and suggested I move to a rental attached to her home. I gladly accepted her offer. Once there, she invited me to do things, such as tea and lunch, with her and the others who stayed through the winter. I learned that my hostess had lost her husband a couple of years earlier and she had a son about my son's age. We shared our grief experiences and our hopes for our sons.

The pages of my book began to materialize as each day passed. I knew that soon I would have to journey back to the states. I'd been in Europe for almost three months, what had I learned? I still felt unclear about my future yet I was beginning to understand that what I really wanted to do was teach people about transitions. It would be my way of giving back, of bringing meaning to my life.

Creating a New Life

When I returned to the states it was nearly Christmas. The ski patrol man I had been dating picked me up at the airport. I looked forward

Loving All of Me

to seeing him, but from his last letter I sensed something had changed. He assured me all was well. He did confess, however, that he had gotten worried I had found someone else, because the letters I had sent him had been delayed for weeks due to the mail strike in Ireland.

By then, it had been two years since Dennis' passing and four months since I had given up my job. I knew it was time to get back into life. I wasn't sure which direction to take, but I knew that I didn't want to work for the Yellow Pages anymore. I was determined to follow the path of my heart.

I hired a spiritual career coach to help me figure out a direction for my life and I shared my thoughts with her. She encouraged me to follow the call to help others going through deep transitions.

A few weeks later, I decided to move to Bend for a slower life pace and explore my relationship with my boyfriend. Two of my sisters lived there also so I knew I would not be alone. In February, I rented a small cottage on the west side of town and a short drive to Mt. Bachelor where Dennis had died. I knew I had more healing to do there.

That year was one of Bend's worst winters. Every morning I awoke to new snow and had to shovel my way to the car, which was parked on the street. I began to question my move. I still didn't know who I was or what I was supposed to do, which heightened my feelings of aloneness. I wondered, "Will I ever find *home* again?"

Pondering

I continued to work with my career coach in Portland and one day she said, "You mentioned that you'd like to work with people in transition. I am working with a small group here, how would you like to share your experiences with them for a small compensation?"

Wanting to follow my heart, I had to say "yes," but when I hung up the phone, I cried. I was paralyzed by fear and started thinking up ways to get out of the commitment. I knew deep down that I had to face my fear. After much trepidation, I put a presentation together.

I traveled to Portland and delivered my presentation to the group. It helped that it was in the casual setting of my coach's living room. Afterwards I could see its impact on people which gave me confidence that what I had to share was of value. Of course, my coach gave me a lot of praise and encouragement.

Meanwhile, my boyfriend and I continued to see each other, but there was a tension that hadn't been there before my trip abroad. After doing all that work around co-dependency, I wanted to make sure I didn't jump into a relationship I might regret. Now that we lived in the same town I had some expectations on how it should be. Unlike before, he seemed distant and unavailable.

The more time we spent together, the more I noticed how different our values were. I was a dreamer. I had ambitions. And he was content to be a carpenter even though he had a law degree from an Ivy League school. He took good care of himself physically, but I was concerned that he liked to come home after a hard day's work and pop open a couple of beers. The tension between us grew.

We agreed to work with a counselor to see if we were compatible. I was grateful he was willing to explore, but it fizzled out after a few weeks.

41

In the spring, I went to visit my parents because Mom was having surgery. While there, I received a call from my boyfriend. He told me that he had met someone while I was in Europe and they had been dating this whole time.

I was livid! Why hadn't he told me in the beginning? Why did he dump this on me when I was visiting my family and couldn't even talk openly? Obviously, I still had a lot to learn about relationships. I returned home to learn that he and his new girlfriend had moved in together. Here I was again: sad, confused, and even more alone.

I prayed and wrote in my journal daily, asking for guidance. I desperately wanted to live from my heart in co-creation with the Divine. I knew I wanted a relationship, but I wanted it to be a conscious one.

The work piece continued to be confusing. Creating a speaking/ teaching career around transition seemed scary so my coach suggested that I begin by teaching at community colleges and speaking at churches. I developed classes such as *Living with Vision* and *Managing Change and Transition*, created my own flyers, and distributed them around town. Looking back now, I don't even know how I had acquired those skills or ideas. I'd only ever taught aerobics classes, certainly nothing like that.

The Yellow Pages, my old workplace, asked me to speak to their organization about change and transition and offered to pay me a fee. I was even more terrified since these people had been my peers and I would, now, be standing up in front of them as an expert. I knew I had to show up. That was the way to following the path of my heart.

In June, I attended a six-week Hospice Grief Group. Afterwards the facilitator asked if I would be willing to lead grief support groups myself. I said I would.

In the grief group, I met a woman who was going through a divorce. She was a storyteller, voice teacher and musician, and she had a group of women friends who was exploring *the feminine* and the Goddess. She lived a couple of blocks from me, so we quickly became good friends. She invited me to some of her groups,

Queen of the Night

and soon (because Bend was still a small town), I began to find a community of like-minded souls.

She also introduced me to a church called Awareness Center that had speakers each week and she suggested I speak there. Through the church, I met a woman who was a hypnotherapist and a dancer. She was a former nun and was always looking for creative ways for people to explore their spirituality. She knew that I was trying to get out and speak so she suggested that we collaborate to create a grief presentation that included movement. I would present a talk entitled "Dance with Grief"; afterwards she would join me dressed in a black leotard and, with music that she had selected, we would dance to the emotional aspects of grief.

The presentation was well-received. The audience was clearly moved. The next day I ran into a few of the people who had attended and they said, "I don't know what you did yesterday, but I have not been the same since."

It was then that I knew, if I was going to impact people, I needed to be more conscious about what I was doing. I needed more education.

Emerging

Through these presentations at the Awareness Center, I met a lot of people. One day an older man named Holy asked if I'd like to attend a Summer Solstice party, held on a ranch outside of Sisters. He attended the presentation previously and thought I might enjoy an outing. He said there would be African dancing lessons and a Reggae band in the evening. It could be fun.

Holy was once a former football player and had been a college career coach most of his life, so he was easy to talk to. He was older than me, and had a big presence. He stood over six feet tall, sported a gray ponytail that hung down his back, and wore a Fedora. Although I felt uncomfortable and shy, I decided to say "yes" to the invitation.

At the party, Holy introduced me to a cute guy named Randy. Randy was a counselor and musician who worked with young adults in the area. For some reason, Holy decided to play matchmaker between us. He said, "Do you think that guy is cute? You would tell a fella if you liked him, wouldn't you?" And he did the same with Randy. Somehow, it worked. Randy and I ended up dancing all night surrounded by little kids. It felt like magic. At the end of the evening we went home together—something I had promised myself I would not do.

Randy called the next day and the next. The more we hung out, the more we liked each other. He'd been through his own dark night of the soul, so he understood the passion I had for working with life transitions. He was charming, cute, talented, creative, and spiritual. Could I open my heart again? I prayed for guidance. Relationships were both exciting and terrifying for me.

He was so easy to be with that I just sort of slid into it. We shared similar values and philosophy. He played in a marimba band, sang, played guitar, and conga drums. No doubt he was highly creative, which was attractive to me. Through his connections, I became even more immersed in the 30 to 40-something crowd and by the end of the summer, I had a community again.

Sometime in our whirlwind romance, Randy began to do some acting with a woman who was in town for the summer, and he simultaneously fell in love with her. Wow! Did I have a lot to learn about relationships! I told Randy I couldn't be with him, but he wouldn't go away. I was relieved when he took a group of young people on a wilderness expedition because I needed time to think. But even from the wilderness he managed to send me a love letter and a dozen roses.

A few weeks later the other woman returned to her home state. Randy still wanted to have a relationship with me, but I was ambivalent. I didn't want to just give myself away. I had a calling to create work out in the world that I did not want to abandon, however, I also wanted love.

After much discussion, I decided to remain in the relationship, even though Randy was unable to let go of the other woman in his mind. Often, he fell into fits of confusion. Despite all this, I stayed.

I had a knowing within me that Randy and I were supposed to be together, and that someday we might even work together. I also felt intuitively that I had something to learn by staying in our relationship, even though it made no sense whatsoever.

We held the tension for a year. Since he couldn't let go of either of us, I suggested he visit the other woman. Although he was scared, he went with the promise that he would call every day. Unfortunately, that didn't happen. It got to be so complicated and painful that I finally suggested we enter a relationship counseling process called Imago.

Every trauma of early life
becomes a drama in adult
relationships unless it is
mourned and healed.
This drama is the deepest
shadow of adult intimacy.
~ David Richo, *Shadow Dance: Liberating*
the Power & Creativity of Your Dark Side

Imago therapy is based on the belief that we enter relationships with an unconscious image of what love is supposed to look and feel like, based on our childhood experiences. We attract people who hold both the negative and positive qualities of our family of origin. Conflict is seen as a doorway to healing and growth and can become a pathway to wholeness.

In therapy, Randy and I learned how to listen to each other and mirror back what we had heard and understood through the other's communication. We learned how to identify and ask for what we needed and wanted by using "I feel" statements. Often, our desires were things we had wanted or needed as children, so what we were doing was re-patterning childhood traumas.

Both of us were determined to have a conscious relationship and were equally committed to the process, and for that I am deeply grateful. It wasn't easy, especially holding the tension of not knowing where our relationship was headed and not forcing our outcome.

All is Welcome Here

Weeks later, it became clear to me that I was no longer willing to abandon myself. "I don't need to be in this relationship with you," I said. "I do not deserve this and I am leaving." The truth came from a deep knowing inside. I was confident that I could now stand in my truth and Randy knew it, too.

Love yourself and everything else falls into line. ~ Lucille Ball

Instead of drawing us apart, it allowed Randy to find his truth and face his fears of commitment and abandonment. A couple of weeks later, Randy asked me to marry him.

Becoming a Facilitator/Teacher/Healer

During that year of our relationship drama, I decided to pursue a master's in Transpersonal Psychology (a form of depth psychology). I chose to study on-line because I didn't want to move elsewhere to further my education.

Transpersonal Psychology attracted me because it included spirituality and the arts along with traditional forms of therapy. It gave me an opportunity to learn about spiritual crisis and healing, creative expression, women's studies, shamanism, shadow work, and archetypes—things I'd been introduced to on my journey through grief. These subjects seemed much more interesting than traditional psychology alone.

The curriculum was a match made in heaven. Most of the modalities included writing about my experiences. How had I formed my spiritual beliefs? How did meditation affect my life? How had I become a woman? What were my feelings and how might I express them through clay or some other form of creative expression? What was a

spiritual crisis, a dark night of the soul? What was happening in my dreams? What myth was I living and could I accept the polarities of living in the human experience? What was the feminine and the life/death/rebirth cycle? My studies became a self-exploration that not only made me conscious of my story, but of our collective story; how the inner and outer impacted each other, and the importance of finding a story that included the body and the earth.

If someone had told me that I would be on this path, when I was working in the corporate world a couple of years before, I would have thought they were crazy. I couldn't have imagined it.

I traveled to the campus for a week-long intensive twice a year. The rest of my studies were done through weekly calls with my mentor. At the intensive, I was exposed to a wonderful teacher named Angeles Arrien. She was a storyteller, anthropologist, and brilliant woman. I wanted to be a presenter like her. I loved her storytelling abilities and her feminine style of teaching. I even contacted her once to see if she would be my mentor. But I shied away when I learned it would mean traveling to her events. As I look back, I wonder if this was one of those lost opportunities. Perhaps I wanted love more than I wanted to be a presenter, or maybe I was afraid that her world might change mine.

In the second year of my program, I took classes in women's studies. I realized that I really didn't know what it meant to be a woman, even though I am a woman. I had questions about who I was and who women in general were; and I was deeply curious about the path of the feminine. Through these studies, I discovered the work of Marion Woodman, a Jungian Analyst and author, who wrote about women finding their true selves by healing both the wounded feminine and masculine within them.

Her writings intrigued me so I decided to interview women and write my thesis on *How Women Come Home to Their Authentic Selves.* I interviewed women in my community and elsewhere who claimed to be in transition. What I learned was that the process included loss and grief, and for most women, it meant finding what Ruth Anderson called, "The Feminine Face of God" (she wrote a book with that name). Women were hungry for a life that included a feminine spirit and were longing to express the truth that was in them.

Stepping Out

I was with my mom and one of my aunts when I was reading Anderson's book. My aunt, an avid reader herself, asked what I was reading. When I said, The Feminine Face of God, she replied that the book looked interesting and said she wouldn't mind reading it. But my mother looked at me with horror and exclaimed: "Oh, you're not going to go there, are you?" In her devotion to Catholicism, I'm sure the very thought seemed like heresy.

In my thesis work, I learned that it was important for women to individuate from their mothers and explore the impact their fathers had on their lives. Our beliefs of what it means to be feminine and masculine come from them, as do our thoughts about God and the Goddess. It was clear that for women to find their authentic (or true) selves, they needed to be able to find what was true for them based on their own inner knowing—which meant letting go of what they thought was the *truth.*

I also took a self-esteem facilitators' training course from Jack Canfield, co-author of the now famous Chicken Soup for the Soul book series. At that time, he and Mark Victor Hansen had just released their first book. In that training, I learned how the inner oppressor lived in me and voiced itself through my own thoughts.

Sometimes it presented itself through attacks on my body and on my creativity, including my writing. Even though I knew it was important to finish the book I started while in Europe and get it out into the world, I was crippled by my own self talk. I would never be good enough as far as I was concerned.

Healing Body/Mind/Spirit

Because my body was in constant pain due to the breakdown it had experienced in my early grieving period after I had the flu, I sought body healers, too. Somatic healing was another aspect of my Transpersonal Studies. I worked with a yoga therapist who asked me to get into certain yoga positions while paying attention to the images that emerged from my body. I discovered that the musculature of the body holds our life traumas and through body work, those traumas can be released. I explored Rolfing, the Alexander Technique, chiropractic work, and nutritional counseling to heal my body aches and my life. I was determined to feel healthy and whole. At times, it seemed like a never-ending process. But

I was undoing years of enculturation, trauma, and abuse that had been inflicted upon my body and soul...and it was something that could never be accomplished through a quick-fix.

One of the workshops I attended claimed they could teach me to sing in a weekend. I was terrified at the thought! Singing in front of a group of people was my worst nightmare. *How could I do that?* But, truth be told, if I wanted to have a voice in the world I had to be comfortable standing in front of people expressing myself.

During that workshop, I came to realize how constricted my voice was. It seemed to be as shut down as my writing; I wondered if both were connected. My friend and neighbor, who I'd met through the hospice group, later suggested I take voice lessons from her. For several weeks I practiced musical scales and learned to open my throat chakra which is a place of energy and from where we learn to speak our truth.

One day she exclaimed, "You know what's the matter with us, don't you? We didn't get enough lap time!" She then suggested we incorporate lap time into our work together to re-mother ourselves and heal the wounds of our inner child. So, we did. We both learned how to receive holding and love from one another in a healthy and safe environment.

Medicine Woman

Little did I understand then the importance of what we were doing; we were unconsciously but instinctively birthing ourselves into wholeness.

I also attended a dream group led by a therapist. We gathered in a circle, talked about what was happening in our lives, and then shared a night dream. After each woman expressed her associations to her dream, the group was invited to share what the dream symbols meant to them. I often left the group thinking, "Who needs drugs when we have the world of dreams?"

My work with dreams took me to Arnie Mindell's Process Work, where I learned how to explore dream images that arise through the body; and Neuro Linguistics with Lindagail Campbell, who taught (through the work of Bandler and Milton Erickson) even more skills to re-frame the stories we tell ourselves. My experience with

Lindagail connected me to the world of storytelling and helped me develop my own skills as a storyteller. Although I was not the director of my life, I spent my time intuitively following the path on which my heart was leading me.

I learned how to pay attention to my inner messages and the world around me, much like a shaman does. On a visit to the Oregon coast, I went for a walk and had a feeling I was going to find a special treasure. I was curious about what it would be. About half-way through my walk, I encountered a seal that appeared to be stranded on the beach. I thought she might be in distress so I reported her to the port. "Thank you," the man said. "It's calving season and many cows come ashore to have their pups. We'll be sure to check on her." The image of that seal cow stayed with me for days and it was far more precious than any agate I might have found.

When I returned to Bend, I shared the story with my yoga therapist. She said it reminded her of the "Sealskin, Soulskin" story in Clarissa Pinkola Estes' book, Women Who Run with the Wolves. I got the book and I read the chapter about that story - the message of that seal cow on the beach was clear: "...our *wildish* nature is to go home again, to feel our fullness, our wholeness." I knew I was on the right path, that I was connected to something larger than myself—something that was continually informing my life. By learning how to listen and pay attention, I remembered again what I had intuitively known as a child: *the world is alive and is always speaking to us.*

God speaks to us every day only we don't know how to listen. ~ Mahatma Gandhi

Bringing Back the Treasure

Randy and I were a good match in many ways. He loved teaching young people how to find themselves and discover their gifts. His degrees were in Religious Education and Youth Ministry and Recreation and Leisure Studies, with experience as a recreation and wilderness therapist. His father had been a Seventh Day Adventist minister, so he had grown up teaching and healing others. In his mid-30s when his life seemed to be falling apart, he had a profound spiritual experience. This led him on a seven year journey of self-discovery and a spiritual path that resonated with him.

Through his unraveling and ensuing experiences, he came across many of the same teachings I had. He honored and revered the Goddess, enjoyed rituals, and explored the symbolic world. His journey taught him about deep life transitions and the initiation process. We found that we had a common language and philosophy, based on similar life experiences.

While finishing my master's degree, I worked with people in transition at the college and the Welfare to Work program for the government; speaking, teaching, and counseling.

I wasn't living the vision of my dreams yet, but I knew I was on the right path and that I would continue to learn and grow. My dreams were filled with images of giving birth and having babies, so much so that I thought my dreams were telling me that I was going to have another child. Although a part of me wanted that perfect picture of a mother and father with their child, neither of us wanted to start the role of parenting once again. By that time we both knew we were being called to a larger world service. I was later

The Seeker

greater than ourselves, we also had each other. In our minds that was enough. We were following the path of the heart. We were confident that Randy was recognized enough in the industry to get students. We also believed that our move would allow me to continue my passions of studying, writing, and speaking about the feminine path to wholeness. And so, we entered the next phase of our journey, another cycle around the wheel of life.

Giving Back/Creating Anew

We had friends in northern Washington who let us stay in their extra space while we explored the area for a place to live. Land was cheaper there and we'd be closer to Randy's children who lived in British Columbia—both pluses as far as we were concerned.

relieved to discover in one of Marion's Woodman's books on dreams, that babies, as dream symbols, represent new creative energies that are emerging.

Oddly enough, not long after my marriage to Randy and the completion of my degree, our outer lives began to change. The school for young adults that Randy helped create and where he had worked for several years, was sold to a large corporation. Randy decided he wanted to create a program of his own.

We talked about it and believed we had the skills to create our own life-transition program for young adults. Properties were too expensive where we lived, so we decided to sell our house and move north where property was cheaper.

Like the archetypal fools, we set out without much of a business plan to begin our school. We had a vision, faith and belief in a power

Right away we picked up one student and began to look for housing. Because we no longer had jobs, the bank wanted to charge us an extra $10,000 for a loan. We looked at several places, but could find nothing that worked.

Then, one day, Randy was at the post office talking to the lady at the window about our need for a place to open our program. "My father-in-law has a place to sell that fits what you say you are looking for. In fact, it might be perfect," she said. We contacted him and went to see it. The property had a big home on 37 acres bordered by forestland; it was ideal for our business. "We think this is a little out of our budget," we told the man. But he replied, "You name what you're able to pay each month and we'll carry the finances." We worked out an agreement and

49

were in the home within a week. We were aware of the synchronicity and the blessings that had just transpired.

Since we didn't have a lot of reserve cash, we lived at the ranch 24/7 as we built our program. With one student, we could pay our mortgage and do what we needed, but not much else. Any extra money went back into the program. We were basically living on faith and, at times, it was terrifying.

Our school served young adults (ages 18-26), and their families, who were struggling with the transition into adulthood. Many had grown up in privileged homes, had never been out on their own, were struggling with addiction issues, depression, rebellion and/or may have been one of those kids who was *out of the box* most of their life. These young people came to us for five months; during that time, we did our best to teach them the skills they needed, in both their inner and outer worlds, to step into adulthood. It was rewarding and challenging. We named our school Life Designs and held the vision that "every moment was a teaching moment."

The first year we had four students living with us—three of whom were sneaking around, getting drugs, and showing no apparent interest in bettering their lives. The fourth was a temporary student who was waiting to get into another program. I finally said to Randy, "Either they go or I go." The insanity of living with addicts was more than I could bear. My body ached from holding the stress of living in that insane world. When the holidays came, we let them all go. We went to dinner and tried to figure out what to do next. We had given our best and failed.

When we returned home that evening, there were lights on in our house; people were sitting at our table. The young man who had stayed with us temporarily decided that he wanted to work with us permanently after he had interviewed the other programs. Randy and I looked at each other and said, "I guess we're back in business!" We learned to trust the ebb and flow of something *bigger than ourselves* at work in our lives.

Within two years, our program grew to the point that 8 to 13 young adults were living with us, so we hired our first staff. Randy and I worked well together, but there was absolutely no separation between home and work. Even when we eventually got a space for weekends, the work seemed to follow us. My dream of writing a book and continuing the work of the feminine seemed to have vanished as I put all my energy into the work in front of me.

The foundational principle for our program was love. Sometimes young people came to us with a tome of psychiatric reports that had begun when they were five years old; other times they came with a rap sheet a mile long. Our only requirement was that they stayed because they wanted to change.

I am amused at the irony of life. I thought I had broken the patterns of my grandmother and mother, but here I was, living in the wilderness with a house full of kids, just like they had. And like theirs, it was all-consuming work. The only differences between me, my mom, and my grandmother were that I got paid for my work and I had the choice to walk away, if the need arose.

By the end of six years of service, I was exhausted and I started to fall back into my own addiction patterns. I knew I had to get out of there and pursue my own dreams. Randy too was tired, although he was *king* there and adored by all. We all loved and honored the magic, dedication and love he brought to the work and we were by his side, serving and helping to build his vision. I lost myself in the process.

We were very fortunate that our first employee wanted to buy the business. Nearly seven years after its inception, serving hundreds of families, we sold Life Designs to him and began another cycle of our lives.

Another Loss of Self

I longed to return to my dream of becoming a published author and sharing my story and experiences of the feminine path to wholeness. It was a part of my life's mission that remained unfulfilled. I needed Randy to support my dreams just as I had supported his, but instead of remembering our agreement, Randy jumped into creating new projects and a new school.

I wanted to write and pursue public speaking, I also needed to create an on-line presence, but I didn't know how to delegate or ask Randy for support. Without instruction, he claimed he didn't have a clue how to proceed. That was hard for me to understand, because I stepped up and helped him realize his dream. His lack of support left me feeling betrayed.

Lost Dreams

Ironically, we didn't realize we were in another transition. We were no longer business owners working together for a common cause. I didn't realize how much of myself I had lost supporting his dreams, or how I had projected my gifts onto him.

Our marriage became strained. Randy went his own way, following passions I did not share. Being a preacher's kid from the south, I think he believed, at least on a subconscious level, that a wife was there to serve her husband and his dreams, even though he might not articulate it that way. While he was away, I was on-line, at home and by myself, trying to create a following so publishers would even consider something I might write.

I worked on my book every day, struggling to put together a proposal and muster up the courage to expose my work. Internally, I felt inadequate—crippled by fear, doubt, and insecurity. Depression plagued me. *Why did I have so much trouble believing in myself?*

I hired coaches and took on-line classes, hoping someone would hand me the keys to living my dreams. I tried new things but was unable to follow through as one simple step expanded into hundreds. Surely, nobody would want to read what I had written. I took marketing classes, mission-defining classes, writing classes, all to fill up the *not enoughness* I felt inside and with the hope that I too could live my dreams.

A coach I worked with gave me the name of a New York publisher and encouraged me to have her look at my manuscript. That publisher's feedback was discouraging and only served to amplify the critical voices within my own head. I was so distraught I took my manuscript outside and burned it. I prayed, "God, please take this desire from me! It's too hard!" Of course, the dream didn't die, but a part of me was in danger of dying as I poisoned my own dreams. (Note: The Feminine Path to Wholeness is the resurrection of my original manuscript.)

Heart Wisdom

Life, once again, intervened when a woman who worked in the young adult industry called to say she was in town and wanted to visit. She was starting a program for addicts and wanted to brainstorm ideas. During our conversation, she brought up the work of Marion Woodman and shared with us that Marion had a three-year leadership program. My ears perked up because her work had truly resonated with me when I was studying transpersonal psychology.

Marion was a primary figure in the women's movement and one of the most widely-read authors on feminine psychology, psyche, and soma. Marion believed that healing old wounds allowed for the emergence of new energies, and that the healing of the masculine and feminine within would create an inner marriage that could support creative energies. I knew I had to work with her.

Tracking Your Journey

Change is constantly tailoring us to become all that we are meant to be. It molds us as surely as winds sculpt a tree or flowing waters reshape the hardest rock. Through change we are initiated into higher and higher states of consciousness.

– Gloria D. Karpinski, *Where Two Worlds Touch: Spiritual Rites of Passage*

If you are reading this book, there is a good chance that you have already gone through huge life changes or are involved in one or more now.

Your life changes (divorce, loss, illness, marriage, birth, etc.) are a call to become conscious. From a mythical perspective, they are sacred events calling you to become the heroine of your life. They are the sound of your soul calling you to wholeness, calling you onto a journey, so that you might remember who you really are: a spiritual being having a human experience. Spiritually, they are the call to a deep initiation that has the capacity to connect you to your true self.

By their very nature, life changes pull us into our depths (into the underworld - our inner world) where transformation takes place. There we acknowledge and grieve the death of our old life which is why many resist it. It is painful to undergo the death of an old life and step onto an unknown path without a clue about where that road leads. Yet this is the feminine path: the life/death/rebirth cycle of the Goddess and nature that renews and restores life.

Held In Love

Exercise 1 – Exploring Symbols of Transformation

The butterfly is a symbol of transformation because of the metamorphosis or transformation the caterpillar makes to become the butterfly. After the caterpillar builds the cocoon, its body breaks down into mush before it is re-formed into the butterfly. This is what we go through, a complete breakdown, when we are in a true transformation.

Take some time to do an internet search on the metamorphosis of the butterfly, the dragonfly, and the frog. Capture (write or draw) your impressions in your journal. Notice what you notice. Feel what you feel. Observe how the breakdown of each is so complete that it looks nothing like its original form. This is what transformation does. It changes us from one state to another...into a more expanded and beautiful state with a much larger world view than we had previously. An old form dies and something new is born – death and rebirth.

The difference is that in the human experience, our breakdown happens within us. We grieve, we let go, we surrender, our lives are ashes at our feet, and we are eventually reborn and returned to life in a reintegrated form, one which is less fragmented, more whole.

Exercise 2 - Self Reflection

In your journal...over a period of several days...reflect on your journey. Imagine you are a shaman with the ability to see in the dark, track the steps that brought you where you are today. Now, view your path from this larger spiritual perspective.

- •   What were the events that called you to the journey?
- •   What were the feelings you experienced as you began this journey?
- •   Who were the people and teachers you encountered?
- •   What were the lessons learned, the wisdom gleaned?
- •   What new perspectives did they bring you in life?

Find a picture (or pictures) that represents your life before and after. What has changed? How is your life different?

Suggestions for Expressing Difficult Feelings

With the loss of an old life comes grief. With grief comes anger, sadness, depression. It is important that you allow yourself to feel it.

- • Find music that expresses how you feel and dance your feelings. Allow tears, they act as a cleansing agent. A good song: I am not Alone, by Kari Jobe   https://www.youtube.com/watch?v=bfveawSAHJA

- • Use colored pastels and/or markers to physically put your feelings into your journal. What color is your feeling? What kind of pressure does it have? Express your feelings on the pages of your journal as many times as you need.

- For those wordless feelings, go to a card store and find cards with images that seem to embody what you feel. Take a color copy of the card, paste it in your journal, and then write. The important thing is that you let your feelings be heard. Feel them and give them voice. They are a healing salve that will empty you so you can become whole. Go to my website for a word list of common feelings (see page 6 for details).

- Find support: a coach or counselor who has been there. Make self-care your highest priority. Remember, you are like the caterpillar in the cocoon - much is happening. Develop your own ways to nest and cocoon so your transformation can happen. These changes continue to occur even though they're hidden from view.

Breath of Life

Coming Into Wholeness

Embracing the Shadow

Our shadow may contain the best of ourselves.

~ Marion Woodman, *Coming Home to Myself: Reflections for Nurturing a Woman's Body and Soul*

The first Marion Woodman workshop I took was on dreams. I was star-struck. There she sat at the front of the room, the woman who had written so wisely and eloquently, and who had taught me and so many other women to find our way through the maze of the spiritual journey as we sought to *find ourselves*. She was a little younger than my mother, yet she understood life in a way that my mother never had. With her background in literature, poetry, theatre, dreams, psyche, soma, and Jungian psychology, Marion quickened something in me. I could feel my imagination open and soar as I sat in her presence.

I had come to the workshop to expand my knowledge of dreams, but also to see if the leadership course was right for me, as it would cost much in time, energy, and money. After a week with Marion, I was assured it was.

The first intensive in the leadership course was held at Pacifica Institute, the school of Depth Psychology in Santa Barbara, CA. Women came from all over the world to work with Marion. Each one came seeking something in herself. Marion was a pioneer in exploring the archetypal, embodied feminine and believed the soul could be found in the body. This premise was her unique contribution to Jungian Psychology.

57

On the first evening, the staff had us do quick introductions. We were to say our names and share something about our lives. Marion did the exercise with us. When her hands touched mine, she looked soulfully into my eyes and said, "My deepest longing is for this work to go out into the world and touch as many people as possible." She believed it was key to releasing women from the inner bondage that so many felt. By then she was in her early 80s and she needed us to carry it forward. I felt her call.

Marion believed that most women had lost touch with their essence growing up with a cultural one-sidedness that favored patriarchal values, intellectual excellence, and spiritual perfection. According to Marion, Sophia (the feminine face of God) is the receptive being in whom the divine and human meet and she was central to our work. When we connect with our own feminine wisdom, we embody Sophia's magnificence. Sophia's wisdom is a heart connection which manifests through all of nature, including human nature.

Together with her partners, Mary Hamilton (dance instructor) and Ann Skinner (voice teacher), Marion developed the BodySoul Leadership course, weaving together rigorous theoretical material with theatrical experiential work to help us awaken our feelings, body awareness, and creativity.

In the mornings, we worked with the metaphors and symbols from a myth or fairytale which carried the ancient wisdom of how a woman finds herself. Then we worked with the symbols from our night dreams to see what our psyche was trying to communicate about our inner hopes and struggles.

We began our afternoons with dance movement and voice work, before doing specific exercises designed to bring our body and soul together. It was fun, interesting, and often confusing. After each exercise,

we took the energy that had been generated and expressed it on paper with paint or pastels through color, lines, or shapes that represented what emerged from our day's work.

Emerging Feminine

Healing Our Mother Wounds

Our true self may have never been mirrored by another person in childhood. We may have to find it elsewhere.
~ David Richo, *Shadow Dance: Liberating the Power & Creativity of Your Dark Side*

Central to the work was healing the *mother/daughter split*. Many of us had been raised by mothers who were disassociated from their bodies and were wounded themselves. They were, therefore, unable to mirror back our true selves.

In the mothering exercise of the BodySoul work, we learned how to hold a loving presence for each other. We did that by holding space without wanting the person to be any different from who they were. This created the sense of safety necessary for the deep work we were there to do. If a woman could get her body to relax, it could become the loving container of her soul.

Personally, I had always felt that my mother wanted me to be perfect. I never felt I could just be myself, to be fully human, and have both my dark and light sides.

Most of my life I longed for a deeper relationship with her. *If only she could tell me that she loved me, or that she was proud of me.* At one time, I thought her approval would make me happy. I didn't realize until my late 30s that I was expecting her to be someone other than who she was, too.

This epiphany occurred in a hospice training on death and dying. The instructor said, "Sometimes at the end of life, people who are dying will gather family around them and let them know how much they love and appreciate them. They make amends if needed. It can become a wonderful moment," she said.

As the instructor spoke, my mind wandered off. I imagined that maybe on her deathbed my mother would tell me that she loved me and was proud of me.

Then I heard the instructor say, "But most people will die how they have lived."

That would be my mother. She would die how she had lived. She'd never been comfortable expressing her emotions. She didn't have words in her vocabulary like *honey* or *baby* or anything near that. With so many children to raise, her actions and words had been utilitarian, as I'm sure her mother's words, with 13 children, had been to her. To expect her to change now would be unreasonable.

My mother once said to me in my adult life, "How can you think that I didn't love you when I cooked you all of those meals and put good food on the table for you?" That was my mother. I could spend the rest of my life hoping for her to be different, to be someone she was not, or I could accept her just as she was—a human being with limiting beliefs and a story of her own.

I could finally accept that in her servitude to her family, she had loved us in the best way she knew how. She had given her life in service. She had slaved over a hot stove for years, often with one or two babies hanging off her hips; canned fruit and vegetables so her children would have something to eat in the leaner months; and provided the best she could with limited resources. That was my mother. She had given her life to us. *How could I think that she had not loved us?*

That day during the hospice training, I gave up longing for my mother to be different. We could both just be the imperfect human beings that we were. If I wanted the kind of mother that I longed for as a child, I would have to become that nurturing mother to myself. And that is exactly what I began to do in the BodySoul work.

Awakening the Creative

Each afternoon in the BodySoul work we danced, an exercise to explore our bodies. We felt what it

Fully Embodied

were stored in our bodies, helping to free us to live authentic lives. We began to grow the courage to assert ourselves and stand in our truth. And next, we did a guided visualization to relax the body and open to the breath.

Once we quieted our minds and bodies, we worked in the deeper symbolic realms which often brought up old trauma or repressed gifts we didn't know we possessed. We transferred the energy to art. I didn't know how to draw, so I took the pastels and poured my feelings onto the paper. Somehow, images began to emerge.

One time, some fish appeared on the page. Afterwards one of the teachers asked me if I was an artist. I replied, "No!" She said, "Well, we're not supposed to comment on the art, but there is such symmetry and rich color here. It must be one of your innate gifts!"

Did she say one of my innate gifts? Could it be?

Going Deeper

Another afternoon during the workshop, a picture of a woman appeared in my creative expression. When I saw her, I knew that she was my *creative self*. I was filled with excitement! *Here she was!* I instantly loved her. I knew she was an essential part of me!

I wish I could say that I went home and immediately made art a part of my life. But discovering my *creative self* was only the beginning. Although I played in the arts at times, I found it hard to make it a priority.

About that time, however, another event convinced me that I had to make artwork an essential part of my life. My husband was associated with a woman named Dr. Arlene Taylor who did brain testing using the work of Dr. Katherine Benziger. She believed that

was like for our bodies to take up space, to reach down to the earth, to open our arms to the heavens, and connect with and interact with other dancers. Through movement, we experienced the joy and miracle of the body – we released the old blocks and opened ourselves to long-held feelings.

Next, the voice teacher led us through sound and breath exercises. We experienced how an embodied sound, rooted from our bellies, had the ability to connect us to our true selves. In opening our voices, we learned to give voice to the memories that it was important to live out of the side of your brain that was your dominant lead, the way it was designed to operate from birth.

I took the test and found out that I was as creative (right-brain-lead oriented) as my husband. Due to my early life experiences, I adapted by using logical, analytical, and objective methodology (left-brain skills). Taylor claimed that my depression was the result of not living out of my primary brain-lead, my natural creative and intuitive self.

When my test results were returned, she informed both Randy and me that I needed to do more right-brained activities if I wanted to live a healthy and balanced life. Otherwise I'd be in danger of imploding upon myself. From that day forward I decided that art-making had to be a priority. It brought me such joy! In my shadow work, I discovered my artistic self.

My family laughs, because I used to proclaim that I was not an artist. Now I have my own art studio. Painting continues to be a way for me to enter the mystery and I never know what new character will emerge. I love every one of them, even in their imperfections. They touch and heal me. I doubt I would ever have found this part of myself without the training of Marion Woodman and the BodySoul program.

Encountering the Shadow

That which haunts us will always find a way out. The wound will not heal unless given witness. The shadow that follows us is the way in. ~ Rumi

Another theatrical tool used in our BodySoul work was masks. During the workshop, we created plaster masks of our faces, decorated them, and then worked with them in the afternoon session. Later, we put on our masks and interacted with each other, letting out any sounds and movements that might naturally emerge. It felt odd initially, but powerful.

One of the masks I created was very shamanic looking. The first time I wore it, it had absolutely no energy. My body felt heavy and I couldn't move. I wanted to hide under a table. Some of the masks were like that, especially if a new energy was just emerging from the unconscious.

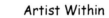
Artist Within

When it was time to interact with the other masks, I danced with a woman who wore a mask that looked like a shy, unloved, adolescent girl. As I was spinning around I felt like a character in Beauty and the Beast. I recognized both masks represented two parts of myself that needed to be healed. That's what the work was about: Learning to love the unloved and abandoned parts of the Self.

As I worked more with my shamanic mask, it began to reveal its gifts. It became more like the Wise Old

Shaman

Man archetype. It revealed that it had much wisdom to share with me. Each time I wore it, I learned more about it and, as I did, it began to transform. One time, I discovered that it was like the Tin Man in The Wizard of Oz. There was a wound that had caused it (me) to lose heart. Another time, as I wore the mask, I let out a sound of grief that penetrated the room. This was the deep sorrow I felt for the neglect and harm that had been done to the earth. I began to realize that this new voice was a positive masculine part of myself that was making itself known in and through me via the mask.

In yet another dance, my mask embraced another dancer who wore a mask that looked like an outcast woman. I realized later how I had begun, through that action, to embrace the outcast woman within myself. *I was becoming whole.*

The Inner Child

Befriending the shadow is really about learning to love. We let the dark out to let love in.
~ David Richo, *Shadow Dance: Liberating the Power & Creativity of Your Dark Side*

Sometimes the work I did in the BodySoul training was a painful resurrection of sadness and grief as I retrieved the lost parts of myself. This was especially true when I connected with the child-like aspects within me.

The first child-like mask I birthed was the *sad inner child* who felt so unloved and unseen that depression and loneliness were her constant companions. Like Cinderella, I knew I was a precious princess, but no one else seemed to see me.

In the BodySoul work, we learned to hold and contain our pain, so that we could create a new story. At first, the young part of myself didn't trust that I'd be there for her. I couldn't blame her because I had abandoned her so many times throughout my life.

However, I recognized this part had healed when, a year later, another child-like part emerged. This time it was the *magical precocious child*. She was the opposite of the sad child. She was loud, boisterous, full of wisdom—an old soul. The sad girl had been her opposite and, the one I had lived out of most of my life. Through the BodySoul work, I came to understand that both energies lived within me. When the magical child was hurt, she could become the sad, wounded child.

Coming Home to My Body

The mind's subjugation of the body can be another ploy of the ego to keep us divided against the Self.
~ David Richo, *Shadow Dance: Liberating the Power & Creativity of Your Dark Side*

I hadn't realized how disconnected I had become from my body through the course of my life. Over the years, it was a whipping post for everything I considered wrong with me. I turned to food and alcohol because I did not know how to deal with my pain or my feelings.

I began to understand, as I worked with mothering my internal child, that loving my body was essential to becoming whole. I could see how I turned to sweets to soothe myself whenever feelings would arise. I was committed to making a change. When I returned home from a session with Marion Woodman, I went to see a naturopath. She helped me understand the connection between my longing for sugar and the abandoned parts of myself. She suggested that my craving for sugar was a sign that I needed to pause and feel instead. But the patterns were so entrenched that I could not effect much change.

For the next intensive, I created a SoulCollage® card to represent my compulsive self. It was a picture of a mummified girl on an altar. I named her *Hungry Girl*. She illustrated the girl inside of me who was unsated.

Marion explained that when we overly-identify with one side (either the masculine or feminine principle within us), we lose a part of ourselves which creates an imbalance. This sets up an insatiable craving that must be filled—a craving that can easily fuel addiction.

Fairy Princess

Knowing and understanding these two energies was immensely helpful. I was now aware that if I fell into a paralyzed state, I could access this other part that was full of joy. The energy of the sad child did not have to consume or cripple me.

Feeling the sorrow of the rejected or lost child is a part of the feminine path to wholeness. The parts of the self that have felt lost and unseen need our acceptance and love, drawing on the good mother archetype in ourselves. In our acceptance, we free the rejected parts from the *shadowlands* and new energy is released into the psyche, allowing our gifts to bubble forth.

Because I desired to change, I joined a 12-step program for food addicts where I agreed to give up the foods and beverages that were toxic to me. After a year of living without them, my body began to heal. I no longer ached. The fog in my head cleared. I had energy again!

One day an image came to me of a wounded dog lying in a corner of a room. The dog was in desperate need of care, but when I tried to touch it, it became defensive. This mirrored the wounded relationship I had with my body. I needed to slowly rebuild that trust. Symbolically dogs are known for their undying loyalty, just as our bodies are. They deserve love and respect. Reconnecting to my body became another gift of my healing work.

Completion

I wish I could tell you that the three years I spent in the BodySoul program completely transformed me. It didn't happen that way for me. True, much had changed. But when I graduated, the outer world still had not caught up with all the inner changes I'd made.

I completed the program knowing that working with women and bringing the feminine to consciousness was the work I was here to do. But the question remained: *How do I take it out into the world? How do I reach the people I am here to serve?* I felt like the Handless Maiden. It seemed I had no choice but to wait for the answer.

Uniquely You

Sometimes, waiting for God's timing is one of the hardest tasks. To stay true to my heart and not act until the way is clear—that was the order now. I had to trust that someday the next right step would make itself known.

64

Accepting Yourself

The curious paradox is that when I accept myself just as I am,
then I can change.

~ Carl Rogers, *On Becoming a Person: A Therapist's View of Psychotherapy*

I spent the first half of my life trying to perfect myself. I consumed one self-help book after another trying to fix myself so that I could be loved and be happy. I was always searching, striving to achieve some elusive and ideal sense of self.

This pursuit of perfection started in my early years. I was supposed to be a *good girl* and was taught to smile even when I was hurting. To maintain that persona, I denied much of what I felt and who I was. Yet no matter how much I strived for perfection, I never felt like I was ever *enough.*

It wasn't until my work with Marion Woodman and the gifted BodySoul leadership team that I understood the value of opening to the unacceptable parts of myself. Marion explained that this is when the new energy (the creative life force), the unlived life can be found. In psychological terms it is called the *shadow.* Our shadow contains our unexamined shame and the rejected parts of ourselves, but it also contains unclaimed, positive and valuable, aspects of ourselves. It is in accepting both the dark and light sides of ourselves and our humanity, that we become whole.

Exercise 1 - Create a SoulCollage®

A fun way to explore your shadow is through a process called SoulCollage®. I became a facilitator in 2010 and have found it to be an invaluable tool. SoulCollage® is a creative and intuitive way to explore the story of you and to connect to the dark and light sides of yourself. In SoulCollage®, you create a dreamscape of sorts of your inner world.

Allot sufficient time to complete (approximately 2 hours). This can even be done with kids!

Supplies:

- ° old magazines (you will be cutting out images)
- ° glue stick
- ° scissors
- ° ruler
- ° card stock (5x7)
- ° your journal
- ° overlay frame template

Note: A great source for cardstock is a picture framing store. Ask them to cut matting scraps into 5 x 7 pieces. An optional 5x7 overlay frame may be helpful when making decisions about your card's layout; it gives you a vision of your card size. Download the template from my website (see page 6 for details).

Part 1 - Card Creation:

Step 1. Once you have gathered your supplies, select images that attract you. Try to let go of any intentions of creating *something* and instead allow the images to pick you.

Step 2. After you've gathered your images, see if there is one (or two) you might use for a background. Pull these out. This is your first layer so assume that your other images will overlay this background.

Step 3. Sort through the smaller images and cut out those you are drawn to. Remember, your space is limited (5x7) and you will have to make decisions. Since you are creating a dreamscape, stay away from words as much as possible and let the images speak.

Step 4. Begin to play by arranging the smaller images over your background. Limiting the number of images to 5-7 makes the card easier to work with when you begin the card inquiry step (following). Pay attention to your intuition to see if it needs more, or less.

Step 5. When you are satisfied with your layout, trim your images as necessary and glue them firmly onto the cardstock, making sure to cover the entire back of each image with glue. Rub the edge of a credit card over your images to reinforce the bond.

Congratulations! You should now have a card or two.

Part Two - Card Inquiry:

The assumption is that your card has something to say to you. With that understanding, ask the card questions and let the images in the card *speak* to you through creative inspirations and impulses. Sometimes it's a little hard to quiet the mind. Just pretend that you are a kid again (the one who can pretend she is a fairy princess). You are here to open your imagination … and give the images a voice.

Although the SoulCollage® Process has several questions to ask the images, you will focus on the first question only. It is:

Who are you?
Ask the question, "*Who are you?*" Next, direct your focus back to your card and allow one of the images to say, "I am the one who…" (You'll want to record the responses in your journal so at the top of a blank page write, *"I am the one who…"* Also, make a notation as to the image you are calling upon.) Ask the question to yourself 15-20 times and record your responses. Do the same process with each of the images on the card.

Once you've recorded your responses see if there is a theme or pattern that emerges. In SoulCollage®, it is also assumed that there is a part of yourself that wants time and attention. Notice if the responses seem mostly light or dark.

Next in your journal write the line: *My light side is*: then leave some space. Below it write, *My dark side is:* See if you can identify the positive qualities of your card. If the dark qualities are more obvious, write those down first.

Remember that we live in a world of duality. Ask yourself, "What would happen if these light sides of myself flipped into their dark side?" Ask the card itself for any dark qualities. If it is difficult to find, simply imagine what the qualities would be opposite of the qualities you listed. Write down the opposites. Then ponder a bit on how they have appeared earlier in your life. Recognize that as a human you hold all of these possibilities within you. By making them conscious, you can choose not to be taken over by the darker qualities because you know you also have the opposite quality to call upon, if needed.

I understand this might not make a lot of sense to you yet. If you want to find out more about the SoulCollage® process, go to: www.soulcollage.com where you can obtain more information. If you don't understand it fully, at least you have begun to open your creative juices. The invitation is to allow yourself to have fun and begin to inquire.

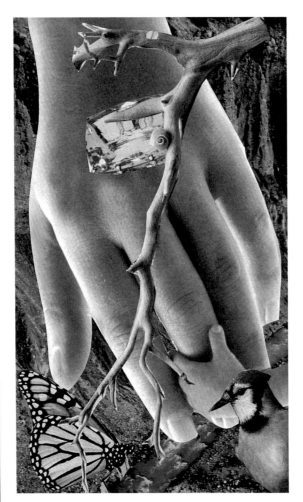

I am the one who: *Is the young creative seed coming from your unconscious...is not fully formed or mature.*

What I have to give you is: *New life.*

What I want from you is: *Your love and support, nurturing, and care.*

How you will remember me is: *Seeing images of young life, whether it is in the form of a baby or new growth in spring.*

My light side is: *I am the bringer of new life and creative energy.*

My dark side is: *I am tender, vulnerable, and easily crushed.*

I am the one who: *Is colorful, spirit-filled, alive, vibrant and beautiful, sees hearts, listens to intuition, flies through the world giving wings to your dreams.*

What I have to give you is: *Beauty, perspective, gifts of the spirit, dreams, ideas*

What I want from you is: *For you to take time, quiet time to listen to me so I can guide you. Allow me to fly into your world to fill your life with the gifts of spirit.*

My light side is: *I am your connection to spirit.*

My dark side is: *I give you too many ideas so fast that you are unable to ground them.*

Lion King

Healing the Wounded Masculine

We must first awaken to our needs,
feelings, and values. Then the masculine
can grow up and say: I shall stand up for
these needs, these feelings, these values.
I shall put them out there in the world. I
shall work with you in all your creativity.
~ Marion Woodman, *Coming Home to Myself: Reflections for*
Nurturing a Woman's Body and Soul

After I had completed the intense three-year BodySoul work, I reflected, "What had changed?" I looked at my life and there was still much that wasn't working. My marriage was in shambles. I still hadn't written my book. I hadn't gotten rich in ten-easy-steps, and I was still struggling with my health and addictive issues.

My mind was filled with doubt. At times, I questioned the sanity of my decision to do the work, had it all been for naught? But I had to trust that it was what I had needed, even though I could not yet see nor understand the reasons why.

My night dreams were filled with raging and wounded men, attacking or provoking fear in me. "Good God," I questioned, "what is happening?" It felt like I was going crazy, that my life would never change. Perhaps following the voice of my heart was a Utopian dream that would never come to fruition.

I thought I knew where I was going...but maybe I didn't. Why was it so freaking hard to get any traction on the dreams I had for my life? It seemed like I was constantly working to better myself. How patient did I have to be? How much faith did I need? I still offered women's retreats twice a year, met with clients, but nothing seemed to really flourish. Could it be that I was on the wrong track?

> *Real inner work requires patience and perseverance; only those who are truly committed will continue to walk the hard and stony path without experiencing obvious results.* ~ Llewellyn Vaughan-Lee, *Catching the Thread: Sufism, Dreamwork & Jungian Psychology*

Then my next step was revealed. In 2010, the year I graduated from the BodySoul course, a masculine figure emerged in my art journal when I was leading a retreat. I did active imagination with him later and he said, "I've been stuck down here for so long even I'm feeling constricted. *Hear me and set me free!*"

It was clearly time to heal my masculine self, to get to know it in its many forms, including how the patriarch lived within me. After all, Marion had said it was about healing both the inner feminine and the inner masculine. Everywhere I looked, whether inwardly or outwardly, the message was the same: *Nowhere did I seem to have a healthy relationship with the masculine.* It was time to bring this part of myself to consciousness.

Removing the Patriarchal Mask

When it came to birthing my dream of becoming a published author, I was like the wounded men in my dreams. I was impotent. I didn't know how to create my vision or how to stand up to the voices in my head that mocked me ruthlessly, "You're crazy! No one will want what you are offering! You'll never make money!"

Individuating

Yet I wanted to serve, make a contribution. I knew I was here to help restore the balance of the feminine and bring soul back to the culture. I knew that women's gifts and voices had been ignored in our patriarchal culture where the focus is on money, knowledge, fame, and recognition. I felt my purpose was to help women awaken to their gifts and I, in turn, had to live mine. To abort my dreams would be a betrayal to myself, my soul, and the world's soul.

Bringing consciousness to the soul confronts the wayfarer with a collective culture, its language and thought-forms that have for centuries rejected the sacred in favor of the rational and material world.
~ Llewellyn Vaughan-Lee

In my 30s I took a speaking class from a man who told me that I couldn't make money talking about things such as spiritual transformation. He said, "People just don't value it." But I believe in the laws of manifestation and that with God, all things are possible.

I would not give up and I would confront my inner tyrant so I could live my creative dreams. I would learn how to set boundaries, value my time, and make my creative dreams a priority. I would wait for clarity, if that was what was needed. I would not react from fear. I would wait and take only inspired action.

One of the reasons I was in such conflict with my husband was that I had spent seven years helping him build his dreams, and now he seemed unable to do the same for me, even though he had mentored hundreds of young people to believe and live their dreams. He needed clear instructions, he claimed, but I could not give him what I did not have.

To heal the masculine, I needed to examine the relationship I had shared with my father, other men, my religion, and the culture to see what voices and messages I had internalized. *That was my new task.*

Dad

My Father

Each woman needs to identify herself as distinct from her parents, her job, her friends, her social environment, the guiding institutions that have fostered her upbringing. Very often, a complex constellation made up of these factors will become daimonic masks by which a woman will define herself.
~ Caitlín Matthews, *In Search of Woman's Passionate Soul: Revealing the Daimon Lover Within*

My dad used to laugh and tell his friends that he had all his kids so that he could get his two sons. My eldest brother was his firstborn, then he had six girls before getting another son. Even though his message was meant in humor, it carried a certain value judgment that was typical in the '50s. Male children were more valued.

73

I loved my father but I always felt distant from him, probably because I had so many other siblings who competed for his attention. I was often left on the sidelines, participating as an onlooker, rather than as the focus of his attention.

He told us kids stories of his childhood, about how much his mother hated him. He said that she sent him to work in the fields just to get rid of him; that she yelled, screamed, and beat him at times. It was so bad that by 8th grade, he quit school and ran away from home. His four sisters confirmed, "He's not making that up! Our mother hated boys." Yet we felt that what he said his mother did to him, he did to us also.

Dad was the rule-enforcer. If we got into trouble, Mom would say, "Just wait until your dad gets home!" Once several of us kids got into trouble and I hid behind the chair so I was shielded from the wrath to come. Directly above me was where the leather belt hung, right next to the silver crucifix of Jesus dying on the cross. Ironically, I internalized that wrathful image—not only of my earthly father, but of God the father as well.

My dad was a blue-collar worker. When I was young, he and one of my uncles ran a sawmill until it burnt down; they lost everything. After that he became an accountant for a logging company, even though he only had an 8th grade education.

According to my dad's sisters, Mom was the only woman who could handle Dad because of his bad temper. One moment he was kind and loving; the next, he erupted with curses because we had turned off the light switch incorrectly. Mom always told us not to cuss, yet when Dad worked under the car, we heard every cuss word under the sun. We never understood why it was okay for him to swear, but not for us.

Sunday mornings was *Dad time*. He took some of us to early Mass, then came home and made buttermilk pancakes, his mother's recipe, which we smothered with butter, fresh cream, and sugar. Sometimes he helped Mom brush some of the girls' thick, curly hair; he was so gentle. Mom, on the other hand, ripped through our curls despite our tears, just to get the job done. While the second group was at the later Mass, Dad played polkas and we danced around the living room. We loved Sunday mornings; Dad was playful and warm, and we felt loved.

When I was in the seventh grade, Dad became City Manager which required that he get his GED. He loved learning and he aced every class. He ordered books on art and literature. I loved these aspects of my dad. It seemed that, as City Manager, he had finally found his place in life.

Dad took some of us for bike rides on the weekends during my teenage years. If I stayed out late, he went looking for me to bring me home. He didn't abandon me when I got pregnant. Despite these caring actions, I don't think I ever really understood or accepted his love for me. I struggled with feeling loved by him even though he was always there for me.

After I became an adult, Dad and I often talked and he was open (to a point) to hearing my ideas. I remember a time when we were discussing the sexual abuse that my nieces had suffered and I said, "It would be helpful if we could talk to the abuser so that he could hear how his actions had impacted others. I think honesty and vulnerability could be healing." Dad exploded into a rage: "To hell we will!" he said. "I was abused by a neighbor boy and we will do no such thing! *Vulnerability is not a good thing!*"

I was in my 40s at the time and had never heard the story of his abuse prior to that conversation.

I wondered if my siblings had. Did my mom know about it? It explained so much. He had been deeply wounded as a boy, and, unlike me, he hadn't had the benefit of counseling and support. I'm sure it contributed to his frequent rages and dramatic mood swings.

My dad surprised us all by how calmly he accepted his diagnosis of cancer at age 82. He seemed strangely relieved. Finally, he was going to see his father in heaven. What I didn't know was whether it was God the Father he longed for, or if it was the father he'd lost at age 4. We girls had always dreaded that moment, thinking he would be a terrible patient. But he accepted death with open arms, deciding for himself that he would die at home, thereby showing us how graceful an intentional death can be.

Two weeks before he died, my youngest sister and I made a trip to visit him. Somehow a conversation of faith arose. My sister and I were no longer practicing Catholics and were the most *New-Agey* of the bunch. Again, something we said struck my father wrong, prompting him to declare, "Well, I guess I won't be seeing you two in heaven!"

My youngest sister was stunned. She felt totally rejected. By then I'd had enough therapy to take a breath and I could see he was the one with the limited narrative. My own spiritual views could and would hold both him and me. I understood he had stated his beliefs and he would not abandon them at death. But he had no idea how his words affected his daughters.

When we returned to his deathbed less than a week later, Dad apologized to my sister, but not to me. Maybe because she had such a violent reaction and was so visibly crushed. A few hours later he went into a coma and in the morning slipped quietly away while

I held his hand. And that was who he was. He could lash out in anger and then, apologize when he was wrong.

Although he was no longer present in the physical sense, I knew his spirit lived within me along with the incongruencies, the judgments, the beauty, and the mystery of his dual nature. In some ways, he was more feminine than my mom. He was connected to his night dreams. He cared about people, especially people who suffered. He was someone who felt deeply. He was a dreamer...and he was an idealist.

Dad served in World War II and sometimes when I was out in the fields with him, he would stop and say, "I believe there will come a day when men will put down their weapons. They'll just lay down their arms." He made me believe it was possible too.

As his daughter, I had inherited both his unhealed wounds and his gifts. I too was a dreamer, a believer that change was possible. Like him, I loved to read and spend quiet time alone. I liked books. I liked learning. I knew how to stay the course; to overcome adversity.

But like him too, I suffered from depression and at times felt the weight of too much responsibility. I could get angry when I let things build up and I could kill my own ideas for being too far out there. I was a walking paradox, just like Dad. I realized instead of being a god, he was a human, like me. In our humanness we loved each other, and in our humanness, we would forgive.

Father Church

I was raised a Catholic, indoctrinated into a religion with an obvious male hierarchy. It was clear that men were the leaders, the holy ones, and that women were the servants whose job it was to wash the altar cloths, clean the pews, cook the breakfasts, and serve the priest. In the early days, it was the priest who led the mass, men who read the liturgy, altar boys who assisted the priest, and men who circulated the collection box. Nowhere was there a model of what a woman looked like in her full *feminine power* and voice in service to the divine.

The nuns wore habits that covered their bodies and hair. Their job was to teach the catechism and, at times, perform outreach. The Virgin Mary, an aspect of the feminine, appeared in the stories but to my young mind she seemed so pure, that no earthly person could live up to her example. She seemed removed from life in the flesh. We were taught that she had conceived without sex and remained a perpetual virgin. Still, her life seemed full of fear, pain, and sorrow. Who would want all of that? But now that I've lived and matured, I can see how her story has lived in me.

Through the myth of Adam and Eve, I was taught that women were the temptresses who led men astray, that bodies were shameful and needed to be covered. By age six I learned that I was a sinner and needed to confess. *Confess what?* At that young age, I didn't understand, so I made up lies just to have something to say.

In catechism, I was taught about heaven, hell, and purgatory. I was told that very few of us would ever

make it to heaven. I was taught that Catholics were the ones with the truth. Marriage with someone from another religion or race was forbidden. The only way to be accepted by God was to be perfect.

In my teens (during the 1960s, when all institutions were being challenged), I began to question the teachings of the church. But it was a closed system and did not take kindly to such questioning. They were the authorities of life, like my parents, and it was my job to obey! Yet it didn't make sense to me why women couldn't use birth control pills, when having so many children was clearly not a healthy—or responsible—thing to do. I didn't understand why I had to have someone outside of me tell me the truth when God was in all things. Why did we have to wear doilies on our heads? What in the world was I supposed to do if I accidentally ate a bite of a hotdog

In the Arms of the Mother

at the game on Friday night, in the era when eating meat on Fridays was considered a sin? How could I measure up to such strict standards of perfection?

In my mid-30s, I could no longer attend church just to please my parents. I felt I was compromising my integrity when I said certain prayers, so rather than practice rote rituals, I took another path in my spiritual life. I chose a sacred practice that was based more on love and compassion, and less on guilt and shame.

If women are to pioneer a new way of embodying spirit in the world today, one thing seems certain: we must listen to the deep source of wisdom within ourselves and tell the truth about our lives and what we are learning. This means questioning everything we have been taught or taken for granted that is not by our own experience.

~ Sherry Ruth Anderson, *The Feminine Face of God: The Unfolding of the Sacred in Women*

I am grateful for my indoctrination in Catholicism, especially the ritualistic pieces of the Mass. I can see that the pathway to wholeness is imbued within its symbolism. There is a virgin birth when we are inseminated by the divine; there is a life/death/rebirth cycle to life, but I didn't understand the symbolism as a kid.

It has been important for me to individuate from church dogma and choose what has truth for me. Finding a loving God and an image of the divine feminine has been an essential part of my healing.

Entering Sacred Ground

School Authorities

The discovery of the authentic self is a long business for human beings. For women, it is lengthened by society's disabling expectations and projections upon women at large. ~ Caitlín Matthews, *In Search of Woman's Passionate Soul: Revealing the Daimon Lover Within*

I started seventh grade in 1968 right after mini-skirts came into fashion. One of the rules in my middle-school was that hemlines had to come down to no higher than three inches above the knee. That rule was reinforced by the male principal who measured any skirts in question with a ruler. If a skirt or dress was too short, the girl would be sent home.

77

In my day and age, men were the principals; women were the secretaries or sometimes teachers. There seemed to be two sets of rules, one for boys and one for girls—especially when it came to sexual expression. Boys were studs if they had sex with lots of girls, while girls were viewed to be sluts or whores for exhibiting similar behavior.

Boys could pursue sports to get into college; young women didn't have a similar option. In my school, girls were not encouraged to dream. Instead, we were guided to develop secretarial skills so we could get an office job, or possibly become a teacher or nurse.

So much has changed since those early days. I am grateful for the work done by all the women before me; they helped make those changes possible. They created opportunities for modern women which, sometimes, we take for granted.

I am also grateful when I see video clips on Facebook of fathers encouraging and reinforcing the image of their daughters as strong, smart, and capable individuals. We have come such a long way, but we still have far to go if women's gifts are going to grace the world.

Be Yourself

Relationships

Bringing the inner masculine to consciousness can help us understand our relationships with men, because we will be attracted to men who resemble our fathers or reflect the image of the masculine we carry inside us. It is important that we understand these early stories, particularly those of our fathers and other male figures from our childhood. Without knowing what we've inherited, we unconsciously attract more of what we've already had in our lives—which is why some women get divorced only

to attract the same kind of man again, in a different form.

When I showed up for myself and honored my creativity, so did my husband. I can't tell you how we got there, except that I pulled back the projections that it was his fault, that he was the one making me feel the way I did. Instead, I focused on what wasn't working for me. I discovered a positive masculine within me that supported what I wanted and needed. I started to love myself and my creativity enough that I was no longer willing to crush or abandon my dreams.

78

<blockquote>
If men and women are to be equal partners in the outer world, the foundations for that partnership must first be laid within themselves.

~ Marion Woodman, *The Ravaged Bridegroom*
</blockquote>

One night I had a dream about a wild man. I was hiking in the middle of a forest and noticed that I was wearing mismatched shoes. The wild man met me, saw that I was in need, went into his warehouse, and brought a matching pair of shoes to me.

As an archetype, the wild man represents an image of the *untamed masculine*. He knows how to follow

Be Brave

the wisdom of his heart, to resist the status quo and create his own path. Following that dream, things began to shift. My workshops filled with ease. I found the work I needed to do. My internal struggles shifted as well. I no longer felt like the Handless Maiden; instead, I felt vital and alive – a woman with two strong hands and two grounded feet.

I stopped trying to change my husband and allowed him to carry his own struggles. I quit raising my hand to be the fixer-of-all-problems and began to follow the joy of my own spirit. I still marvel at how much my husband now shows up for me in tangible ways. He goes out of his way to serve and I don't have to tell him how. I don't have any quick-fix formulas for how we got there. Yes, we did some work on our relationship, but I believe it happened because of my inner healing work and my willingness to take back my projections.

Today instead of a man cave, our home has a woman cave; a basement apartment with an art studio and office where I can fulfill my creative dreams. *Now that is tangible support!*

The Patriarchal Culture and Collective Mindset

Staying aware of how the cultural one-sidedness of the patriarchy influences and infiltrates our lives is a full-time job. That collective mindset rolls out every day on our TV and computer screens, bombarding us with images of what *normal life* is supposed to be. Artificially enhanced images of food, women, cars, money, fame, and fortune flood our brains. Without a conscious filter, we can easily become brainwashed into believing that perfection is what our lives are supposed to look like. Marion warned us to be mindful of the images we take into our bodies; she said it was just as important as the food we consume. She was right.

Most of the images we see are meant to feed our fear that who we are is not enough. They are based on scarcity and meant to entice us to consume. They also feed the desire for perfection—a perfection we can never achieve.

We can buy into those images without question, or we can bring each of them to consciousness so that we can decide for ourselves whether they hold true for us or not. Then, instead of sleepwalking our lives away, we can consciously choose how we want to live life, how we want to impact society, and how we want to honor ourselves and each other.

In the beginning, when you step away from the collective mind, you may feel fearful and lonely. Your mind will most likely shout, "Retreat! Go back!" But once you start to live in harmony with your authentic self and taste what true freedom is, there will be no going back, even though the voices may not go away completely. Daily maintenance will be needed.

Letting Go of Anger

Because of my experiences with the patriarchy in my younger days, I've had a lot of anger and rage. It seemed as though I spent a lifetime overcoming oppression. Sometimes I directed the anger onto institutions (at least in my mind); at other times at men; sometimes internally onto myself and, particularly, my body.

> *They [women] carry in their ancient memories the scars of persecution, and often a deep anger toward the masculine.*
>
> ~ Llewellyn Vaughan-Lee, *Working with Oneness*

I still feel angry with men in positions of authority (in religion and in politics) who have control over women's reproductive rights. I feel angry that women still carry the brunt of responsibility for unplanned pregnancies, while men are not held accountable for their participation. I am livid with those who make the rules, who demand, "You must have that baby!" and, then, turn their heads after a child is born. I feel angry that there is no *real win* for a woman with an unplanned pregnancy— that she is fated to hold the scars for whatever choice she makes even though she did not create her child by herself.

I am angry when I witness authoritative males denying the cries of the earth, choosing economic growth instead of caring for and stewarding the planet. I am upset when I see people and groups of people marginalized and ostracized because they are *different* from the perceived status quo. I am dismayed that we still live in a world that does not see that all men and women are created equally in the eyes of God.

This anger resides deep in my bones, in my gut, and like a war cry, longs to be heard. It is an archetypal rage formed from living in a world where the feminine has not been acknowledged. I recognize that it is a collective wound and a part of the evolution in the story of mankind. No one individual is to blame; men alone are not to blame; rather, both men and women carry the responsibility.

But it is time for change. And that is the reason I've written my story and why I share the vulnerable details of my life with you. Change, *real change*, can only come from within. It's time to heal the wounded masculine. For deep within, we know that we cannot continue to sustain the world in which we live, not the way we're going. We can either wait for the do-or-die crisis to come which forces us to change, or we can begin to work proactively to bring about positive and organizations. Even though men have had an advantage under the Patriarchy, they are wounded as well. It helps to remember that each of us is human.

Change begins one person at a time. It begins by welcoming and making time for the feminine, the symbolic, intuition, and co-creation in our own lives. Change begins by healing the wounds of both the masculine and feminine within us. Perhaps from our place of being healed, we can find new ways of being in the world that are more in balance and in harmony with our planet.

Confronting the Critic, the Tyrant, and the Predator of the Psyche

Until my work with Marion Woodman, I did not know how to honor my creative life. I didn't know how to trust the inner world of the feminine, or even understand what that meant. Every time I tried to write, my inner critic rose up and a chorus of tyrannical voices erupted in my head, paralyzing me, consuming my best efforts. I didn't have a well-developed inner masculine strong enough to stand up for my creative dreams.

Instead of challenging my inner tyrant, or confronting the fears of my inner critic, I colluded with them. I'd been told most of my life that my ideas were too-far-out-there. *Of course, my writing was terrible! Who did I think I was anyway? Who would want to listen to me? What could I possibly say that was of any value? Who cares about this stuff?* I was sure I'd go bankrupt and become homeless, even though at the time I had more financial resources than I'd ever had before. But I believed my inner critics, so I ran from my creative life...and I felt like a coward for doing so.

Spiritual Warrior

changes now—changes that must begin with each one of us.

I am grateful that, having done this work on myself, my anger is healthier. Most of the time I'm conscious enough that I don't react, project, or spew my anger onto someone else. Occasionally I trip up because I'm human. And so are you, as are the men and women we love, our family members, the people in our government, and the leaders in our churches

> *The way to deal with the Inner Critic is not to ignore him but to treat him as any other bully. Stand up to judgmental daimons by commanding them to stop bullying and speak the truth.*
> ~ Caitlín Matthews, *In Search of Woman's Passionate Soul: Revealing the Daimon Lover Within*

No one had ever acknowledged or supported my creative gifts, so I didn't know how to support them myself. Remember, so not long-ago, women had to use masculine pen names to get published and have their work recognized. These memories, and the memories of witches who were hung for speaking their truths, live within our DNA.

When we move forward with our creative dreams, crushing voices will inevitably arise for us - it is the inner critic's job to make sure we stay safely inside the box of accepted norms. If we identify its concern and change that concern into a "how" question that can be solved, the inner critic can become our ally. For instance, if the inner critic says you'll never make money, you might pause and realize that the inner critic is concerned on some level about safety. Some "how" questions might sound like this: "How can I make sure I create safety as I pursue my dream? How can I create income? Knowing what I know, how much risk is reasonable?"

When we collude with the critical voice, it becomes tyrannical. It will chastise us for not standing up for ourselves, thus becoming the predator of the psyche that robs us of our creative dreams.

Co-Creator

Connecting to a Positive Masculine

> *She is lost without an internal masculine, who takes action. The feminine must rely on his focused awareness to fulfill her dreams. Without him, she cannot manifest her vision.*
> ~ Loretta Ferrier, PhD, *Dance of the Selves*

I knew that if I wanted to get my work into the world and be of service, I had to find a healthy masculine. I needed a strong positive masculine within who could help me manifest the visions of my heart. So, I read about the father and king archetype, familiarizing myself with its dark and light sides. To create this book, or anything else for that matter, I needed discernment, focus, boundaries, the ability to show up, and the courage to value my own worth—all qualities of the masculine. I couldn't just work from the feminine side alone. I began, on a conscious level, to call upon my inner king; create a relationship with that part of myself and develop an inner spiritual warrior who could confront the voices of fear inside my head.

It seems that, often, the closer we get to our dreams, the louder those voices become. It may even feel that someone is out to destroy us. We need to realize that it is not the voices outside of us that can destroy us, but our own inner voices. We are the only ones who can kill our dreams.

The Sacred Marriage

> *The heirosgamos, the Holy Marriage, which is the unity of all opposites, is an established possibility - she remembers her true nature. …The current problems are not solved, the conflicts remain, but such a person's suffering, as long as he or she doesn't evade it, will no longer lead to neurosis, but to new life.*
>
> ~ Helen M. Luke, *Kaleidoscope: The Way of Woman and Other Essays*

I discovered that in healing both the masculine and feminine within myself, I was also building a bridge between the opposites. I needed both a healthy masculine and healthy feminine base in order to create.

In psychology and spiritual transformation, this joining of the opposites is called the *sacred marriage*. Out of union, a divine child is born —which is

Inspired Creativity

where the new life force energy emerges. Creation comes out of friction between the opposites. Without the fertilization of the egg by the sperm, there is no baby.

Honoring myself and my creativity will continue to be a dance. There will be times when I won't want to show up to do the required inner or outer work. There will be times when the inner critic will win. But I know they are all parts of myself and that acceptance and love are the transformational work. It is in healing and embracing all parts of myself that I become whole.

83

Understanding and Healing Your Inner Masculine

There is a time coming when a woman's voice won't have to be disguised in a man's garment. Nor will men ever disguise themselves in women's garments. There is such a thing as a human garment. That garment is the inner marriage. The unlived life of men and women will become the source of life when consciousness liberates us from patriarchal power.

~ Marion Woodman, *The Ravaged Bridegroom*

When I was in my early thirties and moving towards success, one of my clients convinced me to buy a pin-striped business suit to wear to work, complete with a little bow tie. She claimed wearing successful-looking clothing would help me become successful.

We can imitate men and create outer success perhaps, but if our dream is to live our own creative life, we need to do more. We need to free ourselves from the inner patriarchal values that keep us stuck and then forge a solid and healthy partnership between our inner masculine and feminine energies. To do that, it helps to understand the qualities of each and provide healing for the wounds each has suffered.

Feminine energy is visionary, creative, expansive, and inclusive but these energies need to be paired with healthy and balanced masculine principles. Creative energy is lost without the action, focus, and awareness to manifest and ground it. Like any relationship, these two sides of ourselves need to be understood and developed.

Understanding this relationship on a conscious level can be quite revealing and healing. In these exercises, focus on the beliefs and the strengths and weaknesses of your inner masculine.

Exercise 1 – Identify Your Masculine Role Models

Supplies:

- ° journal
- ° pictures of male figures in your life
- ° downloadable – Masculine Qualities

In your journal, name the men in your life (your fathers, brothers, grandfathers, teachers, religious leaders, etc.). Think of your first loves. Gather pictures, if you have them. Write your initial impression of each of them and describe your relationship with them.

Then, download the pdf from my website (see page 6 for details) and review the words associated with each. Write those words, as they apply, underneath each person you listed. This process will help you flesh out how each masculine principle lives within you and determine if it is supportive or not. Since humans have both a light and dark side, you will find that to be true of the people who influenced your life. It is part of being human.

Women oftentimes carry the masculine principle, so be sure to apply this exercise to the women in your family too! Do it for yourself as well. Make note of any awarenesses that arise.

Exercise 2 – Explore Your Inner Masculine

Supplies: (refer to Accepting Yourself – Exercise 1) found on page 65

Part One – Card Creation

Cull through magazines to collect images of the masculine, especially those you are drawn to. Create a SoulCollage® card for the images that speak to you most. Follow the instructions as referenced on page 65, but limit each card to two images, a smaller, single image and a background image.

Part Two – Card Inquiry

Next, ask that image: *"Who are you?"* and allow it to respond with, *"I am the one who…"* Ask that question several times. Take notes. Then let the image speak to, *"My light side is,"* and

"My dark side is." As these dark and light sides are revealed, be aware that they may also live within you. How might they play out in your life?

For additional exploration ideas, go to my website (see page 6 for details).

Inner Masculine

AND
BLESSED
Is The
FRUIT

OF
THy
WOMB...

Blessed is She

Tied in Knots

Exploring Addiction

No matter how smart you are, or how much "work you've done on yourself," you alone cannot outsmart the psychic force of compulsion and addiction. If you could, you would have done so by now.
~ Marianne Williamson, *A Course in Weight Loss: 21 Spiritual Lessons for Surrendering Your Weight Forever*

No matter how much work I had done on myself, I still had habits I could not fix with self-will alone. If I wanted to be whole I had to be willing to look at, and come to terms with, my compulsive/addictive self.

In the western culture, most people are addicted to something: money, power, fame, TV, video games, drugs, alcohol, sex, sugar, gambling.... you name it; there are a thousand ways to escape the pain of being human. We are not taught how to deal with our feelings. Instead we are encouraged to escape them.

Spiritually Bereft

As a kid, I did not find a soul connection in Catholicism. A schism occurred for me somewhere around second grade when the catechism moved from "God is everywhere and in all things" to "You're a sinner and must learn to confess!" Questioning our faith was not an option. My mother was adamant that we believe as she did. "If you live in this house, you *will* go to church," she'd exclaim. The church dogma was gospel, as were her rules. We were to obey them and that was that!

My headstrong Aries response to such control was rebellion. If she couldn't handle who I was, I'd go underground and do what I wanted anyway. What did I have to lose? I didn't seem to have a life, at least that's what I thought in my angst-filled teenage mind. Then I found myself pregnant at 17 without a solid sense of connection with a source greater than myself. I was a lost soul.

Addiction History

Compulsions are intricate survival systems that we create because we don't know how to be there for ourselves.

~ Mary O'Malley, *The Gift of Our Compulsions: A Revolutionary Approach to Self-Acceptance and Healing*

In my sophomore year, I stood outside the high school with my girlfriend as she puffed on a cigarette. "Come on. Have one, it's cool," she said as she handed me one. I took a drag and thought I was going to die. It was the nastiest thing I had ever tasted. Nothing seemed *cool* about it, but that didn't matter. I wanted to fit in at any cost. Who was I if I wasn't cool? After all, Cool Cat had been one of my nicknames as a kid.

Another friend and I got kicked off the cheerleading squad that same year because some kid convinced us to take a sip of wine on the rooter's bus. That should have been the wakeup call I needed, but at 16 it became just another reason to dislike the establishment. Unfortunately, I hadn't yet developed the connection between cause and effect; that one sip was a precursor of things to come. When I partied I liked the surreal feeling, the confidence, and the connection alcohol created.

By my senior year in high school, I had every compulsive and/or addictive behavior possible.

I drank and smoked cigarettes and pot on the weekends; had an unhealthy relationship with food and my body; and was into casual sex.

Little did I know, addiction was another part of my Irish legacy. My mom's family was riddled with it. At family reunions alcohol and cigarettes were common; gambling, an integral part of the festivities; and desserts, more abundant than main dishes. Many of my uncles had lost marriages and gotten into trouble with the law because of drinking. The ones who weren't addicted married addicts.

Mom was not an alcoholic but I think she was a food addict. She struggled with weight all her life. I was embarrassed by her at times, especially when she was pregnant. She never bothered to tell us of her condition; we just saw her getting bigger and bigger, so much so that at one point, the kids teased that our last name *Donahuge* instead of Donahue.

For us, sweets were the cure-all, even after we left home. Right after I learned about my dad's cancer diagnosis, I went home for a visit and cried when it was time to leave. Mom walked me to the door. "Do you want a chocolate chip cookie for the road?" she asked. I had to laugh.

My mother was diagnosed with diabetes in her early 50s and my dad was hypoglycemic. Dad made the necessary adjustments, but Mom never could. Even when she had her gallbladder removed, and later had to have two toes amputated, she could not change. What irritated me is that she saw the addictive tendencies in me but was blind to her own and I thought she was a bit self-righteous about it.

Depression was my constant companion and I think it caused me to be more susceptible to addiction. Once as a child, I sat on the bathroom sink, crying in front of the mirror because Mom had forgotten my

Night Journey

birthday. I don't know why I didn't tell her; I guess I wanted to know that I mattered. I didn't know at the time, but she had just returned from her father's funeral. In my mind, she simply didn't care.

When I was 17 and very confused, the town pusher planted some drugs in my locker. I took them home, looked at them, and then swallowed them.

> *Our compulsions serve two functions: the first is to keep unacceptable feelings buried deeply within so we can be numb enough to survive, and the second is to bring us comfort.*
>
> ~ Mary O'Malley, *The Gift of Our Compulsions: A Revolutionary Approach to Self-Acceptance and Healing*

Body Disconnect

> *At the center of addiction, in one form or another, is a radical betrayal of trust. An addiction reenacts a traumatized relationship to the body.*
>
> ~ Marion Woodman, *Ravaged Bridegroom*

I didn't think much about my body until I reached early adolescence when everything changed. In 6th grade, we were dancing in the gym one day. I could feel the music living and breathing in me. I was really enjoying myself, that is, until a girl said, "Where did you learn to dance like *that?*" For the first time, I felt self-conscious, inhibited. And to make matters worse, boys started looking at girls, and girls started talking about boys. It was all so confusing!

My body was changing, too: my breasts budded and my hormones raged. It was no longer okay to run around without an undershirt. I didn't know who I was in this emerging world. Just one year before I played in the woods, an innocent girl, free of concern. Now this! The arrival of my adolescence coincided with our move into town and it thrust me into a new way of life, full of emotions and societal expectations. I was unprepared for these changes.

In high school, girls talked about their breasts and obsessed about how they looked. Our bodies became a source of status that labeled a girl worthy of attention or not. Thin was the rage with 5'6" tall, 90-pound Twiggy as the ideal model. To make matters worse for me, my closest friends were naturally thin. I was not.

Sex, drugs, and rock & roll infected our small town. By then, I was already so confused about the role of my body and so out of touch with my true self, it was just easier for me to disconnect and join the revolution.

The body has been made so problematic for women that it has often seemed easier to shrug it off and travel as a disembodied spirit.

~ Adrienne Rich, *Of Woman Born:Motherhood as Experience and Institution*

Entering the work world after high school only perpetuated my on-going disconnect. I couldn't afford to listen to my body if I was to survive as a single mom. I had to keep moving, keep producing. The same was true for my life in the corporate world. I began my day with a dose of caffeine, pop M & Ms throughout the day to keep my blood sugar stable, drink wine at night to unwind...and then start all over the next day.

The Twelve Steps

It took me years to acknowledge that I was an addict. Certainly, I could control whatever it was, right? I was still highly functioning yet, I put on a few pounds every year. I drank too much! The training with Marion Woodman and the BodySoul work helped me get honest with myself. I finally realized that my body was a sacred temple and, if I wanted to be whole, I had to take care of it.

I resisted the idea of powerlessness. I still did not understand the debilitating nature of soul loss or the power of genetic predispositions. I thought I was weak and just needed to get a *grip* on myself.

When I entered the 12-step program for food addiction, I was ready for change. I couldn't stick to a diet after menopause. I joined Weight Watchers but consumed all my points in fudge bars, popcorn, or Weight Watcher's cookies while the vegetables rotted in the bin. Essentially, I was starving my body. I finally became so desperate that I agreed to give up alcohol, caffeine, flour, and sugar. That commitment was *huge* for me.

There were times I hated going to meetings. It was difficult to surrender to people telling me what to do. With my religious wounds, I had a hard time grasping that there was a God or a Higher Power who cared what I put into my body. I thought I knew what was best for my life, and in most cases I did. But when it came to overcoming years of patterning, I did not.

I discovered, imbued in the 12-step program, another pathway to wholeness. I had avoided the 12-steps for years because I didn't believe philosophically that claiming you were an addict and affirming your lack of power was healthy. My own willfulness had gotten me nowhere yet it led me to seek help. Ironically, the more I surrendered the more grace I received.

> *I finally saw that it was never food that I was hungry for. Rather, what I was really longing for was a deep and abiding relationship with who I truly am.*
>
> ~ Mary O'Malley, *The Gift of Our Compulsions: A Revolutionary Approach to Self-Acceptance and Healing*

Forgiveness of Self and Others

Losing weight and eliminating alcohol in the 12-step program was just the beginning of my healing process. Healing my mental, emotional, and spiritual wounds required real work. There I was, 50-some years old, and I still carried the shame and guilt of my early life choices. I felt unworthy of forgiveness for bringing a child into the world without knowing who his father was.

Centered

I was impressed that my body could heal after so many years of abuse. It gave me hope that someday we can also heal the earth (mother, matter). As with any change, I knew it had to start with me. If I could face my own addictive nature and stop abusing my body, perhaps corporations could stop abusing the earth, too.

At times, I hated having to grow up and take responsibility for my life. But I have found that when my food is clean, my mind is clear and the verbal assaults on my body which run rampant when I am in my dis-ease, go away. Eating right and working the 12-steps has become a spiritual practice that I strive to maintain—a healthy body weight is only part of it. At my age, my health is my wealth. I need a clear body, mind, and spirit to live the life of my dreams.

I was drunk when I told the young man I thought was the father that I was pregnant. He pushed me aside and told his twin brother to take me away. Later that night in my drunken stupor, his brother had sex with me, too. Since my son's birth was past his due date and there was only a month between the two opportunities, there was no way for me to know which one was the father. I eventually found the courage to press the issue when I was in my 40's, but I was told that DNA tests could not prove who the father was with 100% accuracy; the brothers were identical twins. I had created a fatherless child.

I can't begin to tell you how ashamed I was of my actions. For the longest time the pain was so great that I could not even admit it to myself, let alone to anyone else. I still don't like to talk about it. *I mean, who does this?* The answer? People who are young and naïve do this. People who become unconscious through drugs and alcohol do this. *Lost souls, people who are hurting and unseen, do this.*

Healing that part of me has been the work of a lifetime. I've had to accept that I may never find a resolution, other than to *accept what is*—a principle I learned through the 12 steps. Unfortunately, the two young men involved refused to take responsibility for their part. They never offered to get a paternity test to prove that they are not the father (even when I offered to pay for it). In so doing, they denied my son his biological roots.

> *The word resentment means to feel again. Each time we repeat to ourselves a story of how we've been wronged, we feel again in our body and mind the anger at being violated. But often enough our resentment of others reflects our resentment to ourselves. When someone rejects us, he or she might be reinforcing a view we already hold—that we're not good enough, not kind enough, and not lovable enough.*
>
> ~ Tara Brach, *Radical Acceptance: Embracing Your Life with the Heart of a Buddha*

I obviously carried a lot of resentment about this over the years. I hated that I had to be the one to carry all the shame. I hated that the twins didn't have to own their part. I hated that they got to go on with their lives, while I almost killed myself trying to raise my son alone. I hated that I felt so powerless because I could not and will never be able to give my son a father.

Through my searching and fearless moral inventory in the fourth step, I chose to admit that I had created this situation. I made choices that brought me to this place. I abandoned myself, became unconscious, and made poor choices. *I did that.*

In my fourth step work, I shared my story with trusted people and began to heal from the shame. I found the willingness to make amends for my part. It was, in a word, *humbling.* It took me months to be able to do it. A year ago, I wrote a letter to the twins, owning my part and forgiving them. In forgiving them, I found freedom from my own perceived sinfulness, leaving years of my old story behind. The freedom released a new vitality within me.

Again, there is no quick-fix, no instant solution. Forgiveness happens every time that old story enters my mind and I choose to *let go and let God.* I may need to repeat it a hundred times or more. In order to be an empowered woman, I cannot afford to remain a victim of those boys from my past, the church, the principal, or the patriarchy in general. *I must own my part.*

I must also forgive myself for my indiscretions. I cannot become whole if I hold that young part of myself hostage. I love her and I will honor her for her courage. She did not run away from her mistakes, her responsibilities. She stood up and became the heroine of her life. In doing so, she brought me to this place, to a place of wholeness.

AT THE END OF TH AG
Before you appears
a woman with a bucket,
Here you must give up asking,
bend to the water,
lift the old rag.
Wrung dry,
begin here
in this small corner
repetitious
wiping, cleansing,
polishing

Bucket Woman

Loving Myself Just as I am

> *You've been criticizing yourself for years and it hasn't worked. Try approving of yourself and see what happens.*
>
> ~ Louise Hay

I've always loved the scene from the Bridget Jones movie when sharing about the handsome man she's been dating, Bridget exclaims, "He loves me just as I am!" Throughout the movie, she tried to quit smoking, lose weight, and manipulate herself into an outer ideal so that someone would love her. Someone loves her just as she is.

Garden Devi

Empowerment comes when we choose to love ourselves *just as we are*. I think that's really what the 12-steps are about. Once we discover self-love, we find that who we are is enough! And when we recognize we are enough, we rarely cause harm to ourselves or another. In healing ourselves, we heal the world.

Getting Honest

You were never created to live depressed, defeated, guilty, condemned, ashamed or unworthy. You were created to be victorious.

~ Recoveryexperts.com

Do you have a habit you know is destructive that you can't seem to stop? Behaviors you cannot change through willpower, have most likely crossed over into a compulsive or addictive behavior or thought patterns. These tendencies can keep you from stepping into your true and highest self. They can rob you of your creativity and have the power to destroy your life, health, and relationships.

Shadow Self

Nobody sets out to become dependent. Often it occurred because you looked for something outside of yourself to fulfill a need you were unable satisfy another way. But things, or substances, can never free you from the discomfort you wish to flee or fill the longing your soul is trying to express. If anything, over time, these dependencies will only compound your problem. The invitation in this chapter's exercises is to love yourself enough to make your life and health your highest priority.

Unfortunately, compulsive behaviors are like barnacles on a ship – not easily released. To do so requires work and effort on your part, a willingness to build a relationship with a power greater than yourself, and a willingness to take steps and actions you have avoided in the past. Letting go of destructive behaviors can be hard, but it can change your life exponentially.

Exercise 1 - Take an Inventory
Where has your life become unmanageable?

On some level you know when certain behaviors no longer serve you. Notice where you choose to escape or tune out when life gets hard. Pay attention to those times when you say to yourself, "I've been working hard. I deserve _____," or "I think I'll reward myself with _____." Make note of these instances in your journal.

Reflect on the changes you would make if only you could. What are the behavior patterns that are keeping you stuck, limited, or dissatisfied? What are you tolerating in your life? When do you say, "I can't stand the pain, so I will just _____?" What is one modification you could make that might change everything? Do you feel ready? If not, pray for the willingness to change and trust that you will respond when that time arrives.

Treat yourself with compassion. You have done the best you can, but now you have chosen to become conscious. Let your desire to step into your true self become greater than your desire to remain stuck.

Exercise 2 - Find Love-Acceptance-Surrender
Are you ready to try something new?

Supplies:

- paper (yellow pages, newspaper, painted paper, brown paper bag, specialty paper, etc.)
- glue stick
- journal
- scissors

To heal your life, you need to decide that you are willing to do something different. It requires acceptance - acceptance of where you are, where you have been, and a belief that something else might be possible. It also requires you to surrender.

You have probably tried to change, but have been unable to follow through because of the nature of your compulsion. Surrendering to a power greater than you (whatever that is for you) will help. Remember, you are a child of a loving God and your health, life, and relationships are worthy of whatever discomfort you might feel as you change.

In your journal:
1. Using the paper you selected, cut out three hearts and glue them onto a painted page (paint the page as described on page 7) in your journal.
2. On the first heart write the reminder, "*I love myself just as I am.*" On the second one, write, "*Acceptance is the answer to all of my prayers.*" Write, "*I am willing to surrender.*" on the third heart.
3. Jot down in your journal any thoughts that arise. Notice any resistance you might feel. Just breathe and pray for the willingness to surrender.

For additional exploration ideas, go to my website (see page 6 for details).

For additional exploration ideas, go to my website (see page 6 for details).

Interwoven

Bridging Love and Sexuality

If sexuality is one dimension of our ability to live passionately in the world then in cutting off our sexual feelings we diminish our overall power to feel, know, and value deeply.

~ Judith Plaskow, *Standing Again at Sinai: Judaism from a Feminist Perspective*

One weekend when I was 17, a friend invited me to go on a double date to a movie with her and her boyfriend. On the way to the theater, beers were opened and we pulled up to a hotel. I wondered why we had stopped there. Although my friend was with her boyfriend, I was with a guy I barely knew. Suddenly, I realized we were not going to a movie and I was expected to have sex with this guy. What was I to do? I considered calling home, but how could I call home? I couldn't even talk to my mother about getting a bra, menstruation, or birth control pills - the communication gap was just too big. I knew if I called home, I'd get into trouble so I decided to ignore the pain and confusion; perhaps it would all go away. I did what my peers expected me to do that evening, but to do so, I had to detach and disassociate.

I had only explored sex with one other guy up to that point. In the previous instance, we were together and it was consensual. This time was different, though. I tried not to feel anything. Afterwards, I was embarrassed and ashamed so I took another drink and pretended nothing had happened. I felt awkward, weird. As I drank more of the beer, I contemplated what I would tell my mother.

101

I had been in similar trouble before as a five-year old. I was caught under the covers, kissing a boy who was the son of a family friend. I was teased about that one for years.

Then there was the slightly-disturbed neighbor boy who used to scare my sisters and me by chasing us down the back roads near our country home. Mom said she thought his stepfather abused him; she always felt sorry for him. Sometimes when we were outside, that boy would go to the open window above his garage and expose himself. One time when I was on the swing set near his house, he stood directly in front of my swing and exposed himself. My younger sister ran home, told Mom, and I got into trouble. I never understood why I was blamed.

Later. when we were adults, my mom revealed that she used to have the same disturbed boy babysit us. I was shocked! I had no memory of it, but was appalled that she would leave us in his care. Mom told us about another occasion when one of us girls came home from his house without any clothes on and I often wondered if that girl was me. Those memories are a blur or are altogether inaccessible.

But that's the way it was in those days, parents didn't want the neighbors nosing around in their business. Mom coached us to be silent in school about anything that happened at home. It certainly was mums-the-word around topics about sex or

sexual abuse. What was a mother to do? Where was she to find her voice and strength to confront such a forbidden subject, when she clearly didn't have the words? Perhaps it was easier to brush it aside and hope there was no lasting impact on young children. But the truth is, memories pushed into the unconscious of the individual, family, or culture never go away. They follow us through life, generation after generation, until they are exposed and healed.

As I write this chapter, we are in the 2017 Presidential election between Donald Trump and Hilary Clinton and many of these same shadows are

Holy Vessel

rearing their ugly heads. Even now there is a sense of the truth being minimized, pushed down. Beliefs, such as: *boyish locker room talk is acceptable* … and *the truth doesn't really matter*…. and *women are liars and only looking for their day of fame*. But we know that it does count, because our bodies carry the stories.

After that *movie night* spent at the hotel, I became more deceptive and I started using alcohol not as just a way to have fun, but to stave off shame.

Undoubtedly, I was vulnerable to teen promiscuity because of both my early sexual experiences and the '60s culture. I did not know that I deserved to be cherished or that relationship was important. I liked sex; it was fun…and powerful! The woman's liberation movement was at its peak, however, I quickly discovered that girls were not supposed to be *too* sexual. Even though such behavior was applauded for boys, it was still unacceptable for girls.

Body-Soul Split

The difficulty is that, despite these great claims for liberation through sex, more of us still carry in our bodies the inheritance—physical, psychological, emotional, psychic, and spiritual—of at least four generations of women and men whose views on sex were clouded by fear, disconnected from an actual "body of wisdom", and strongly influenced by the culture's perverse and rigid views.

~ Regina Sara Ryan

My mother was unable to provide me with a healthy sense of sexuality. The topic was so taboo, she couldn't even talk about it. Her way of keeping me safe from getting pregnant was to enforce strict curfews, not allow me to date or bring boys to the house. Paradoxically, in her attempt to control, she gave up all control.

She told me after I was an adult that if a woman of her generation didn't have sex with her husband, he could have affairs with other women. Apparently, that was one of the rules of the patriarchy. A woman was to serve her husband, but a husband could legally and morally have sex with another woman if his wife didn't fulfill his *needs*, as long as the other woman wasn't married.

When we were kids, we saw Mom go to her room, put on lipstick, and fix her hair before Dad came home from work. Sometimes we saw them kissing, but other than that we were horrified, like most other kids, to find out our parents had sex.

My mom's views on sexuality were ultra-conservative and she found it intolerable when homosexuality gradually became more *accepted*. Mom felt as if something that went against everything she believed was being thrust *upon* her. It was intrusive to her world views.

I tried to get her to see that for many people, it wasn't a choice. What if she had been born differently, wouldn't she want the opportunity to experience love and marriage? Would she want to live her life in hiding and shame? But she couldn't go there, even though she had a nephew who was homosexual. Any deviance from the cultural norms of the '40s and '50s was just too much.

While I grew up during the liberation of the '60s, my mom's voice, the church's teaching and society's views lived within me. It created an internal split between my body and my soul and left me confused about the role of sexuality. Was sex a sin? Was it okay to have a body and receive pleasure? Was my body something to cause me shame? Should I keep it hidden? Could I trust myself and my sexuality? As free as I was, I could not escape the impact of this early imprinting. I was not free.

> *If our daughters do not learn how to trust their own bodies around sexuality, we are creating another generation of women who will spend most of their adult years trying to re-learn how to feel safe in their own skin.*
>
> ~ Pamela Madsen, *Why Don't We Trust Young Women with Their Own Vaginas? Huffington Post Blog*

At times I dreamed that I was making love and my mother would come into the room—a sure sign that I had inherited a belief that sex was somehow bad. My sexual freedom would take many more years of cultivation.

Sex and Marriage

I enjoyed sex in my first marriage, even though I still carried the shame of having a child outside of marriage. I was afraid of being my full sexual-self, since it had gotten me into so much trouble and had caused such painful rejection.

In my 30s, I felt that my body had to be perfect and that I should try to look sexy. Sometimes looking *sexy* was fun and provocative. But I didn't know how to fully let go, to let myself be loved physically, because my body was filled with so many rules and so much trauma and unhealed shame. I didn't know how to ask

for sexual fulfillment. I didn't even know I had a right to ask!

It seemed that sex was about pleasing men. Most books written about sexuality focused on performance and sexual positions, rather than on creating a loving connection.

Finding time for connection and intimacy was challenging with the two of us working stressful full-time jobs. We went through the motions of connecting sexually, but we were only partially successful. I didn't know how to keep sex fun and alive in our marriage, but I did my best and so did my husband.

When Dennis died, I thought my sexual-self had died along with him. I looked in the mirror about six months into my grieving period and realized that at 36, I was still young and vibrant. I was not ready to live the rest of my life without love or partnership. Connecting to my sexual feelings, and myself as a woman, was the first sign that life might return to me.

But what was healthy sexuality? I didn't really know. I knew I wanted a real connection of body, mind, and spirit. I wanted a communion, of sorts, more than I wanted recreational sex, sexual fantasies, or sexual positions. It didn't mean sex couldn't be playful, but I also wanted mutual caring, heart and eye connection, presence, that's what I wanted— gentleness and *groundedness*. I finally identified what I wanted and needed in my next relationship.

Second Marriage

When I met my current husband, I was clear that I wanted a deep physical, emotional, and spiritual relationship. I was disappointed that we became sexually involved at the beginning of our relationship because I had promised myself that I wouldn't. Even so, I am grateful we had similar values which gave us a foundation upon which we could build.

We had a good sexual relationship in the early years of our marriage, until we created Life Designs and, suddenly, all those young people were living with us. That really put a damper on our sex life for me!! I never felt comfortable expressing myself intimately in that environment.

After we sold our school, I started menopause. By then my youth was fading and my interest in sex waned as well. I didn't realize how much hormones affect sexual arousal. At one point, I wondered if my diminished sex drive was causing a problem in our relationship. The truth is that there were other things going on in our marriage which needed to be addressed.

Randy was experiencing losses and betrayals of another nature and was completely withdrawn emotionally. When we did connect sexually, I felt the weight of his sorrow. It seemed I was the receptacle where he released what he could not handle. That also affected our sexual life.

As the tension in our relationship mounted, I decided to go back to a therapist. I thought if I got honest about my early sex life and the shame I felt, I might somehow be set free. Seeing the therapist and sharing my hidden guilt and shame healed part of what ailed me but other problems remained.

> *To heal ourselves, we need to reclaim our bodies as expressions of God and vehicles of divine life, love, and pleasure.*
>
> ~ Jan Phillips, *Divining the Body: Reclaim the Holiness of Your Physical Self*

As I relived some of my past—the past I had suppressed and drowned with alcohol, those times when I'd been violated or had sex when I didn't know how to speak out—my body recoiled from my husband's touch. I could feel my breath constrict. I didn't want to be grabbed. I didn't want to be approached or surprised from behind. I went into fight or flight mode. I tried to explain to my husband what I needed and wanted; and he took offense, as if I was saying that who he was as a man was not enough. So around and around we went.

We became the typical love-avoider and love-pursuer couple. I had grown up in a large household and had learned to be self-contained. I didn't need a lot of touch. But my husband was the opposite. He was one of three children, the first born. He desired a lot of love, affection, and attention. I talked with my gynecologist about it and she said, "I can't tell you how many women I see in here, going through menopause, who express the same thing."

There were no easy answers. It was clear that we were in another phase of our lives. I tried hormone replacement therapy for a while, but then decided against it. That was only half of the equation. I still had to rebuild my relationship with my own body, as well as work to fix the problems in our marriage.

This coming-together and moving-apart is an on-going dance between men and women. Men connect physically and women connect through the heart. When this is out of balance it impacts the relationship. Sexuality is not static. Everything in our life affects our sexuality.

Another Step to Becoming Authentic

While it was precisely women's sexual power that was venerated and sanctified in the old religion, this power was demonized and denounced under the new patriarchy.

~ Jan Phillips, *Divining the Body Reclaim the Holiness of Your Physical Self*

Listening

Honestly, I did not know what *healthy* sexuality was. I did know that neither the rigid views I had been raised with nor the blatant way I rebelled in the '60s was healthy. In my quest for wholeness, I decided I needed to heal these wounds by attending a workshop on sexuality.

The weekend workshop was designed to help us get to know ourselves as women, fully embodied in our own sexuality. Topics included learning how to ask for what brought us pleasure (sexual or otherwise), learning to honor our bodies, and the beauty of a woman's sexuality.

As the workshop approached, I became increasingly anxious. Ugh, not sexuality too! The voice of the old shame I had inherited said, "There are some things you just don't talk about or share in public." I was about to do both, talk and share. Fortunately, a friend decided to go with me, so I had a touchstone if things got too weird.

I sat like a wallflower at the beginning, shy and uncomfortable. My inner voices, the voices of old, whispered, "Mum's the word!" "You don't talk about this stuff to anyone!" "Put a lid on it!" It took me a long time to feel safe. Once I did, I discovered my anger - anger at my husband, anger at men in general, anger at myself for becoming so disconnected.

I didn't know I had so much anger around my sexual self even though much of my soul-wounding had been to this part of my psyche. I was angry, too, that I always made things my fault when it came to relationships.

I was ready to *bolt* by the second day, but I didn't because I really wanted to learn how to live authentically in my own skin without shame, regret, or anger.

Then the facilitators of the workshop asked us to undress. I was stunned. I didn't know if I could do it, but I'd come there to learn. Each new stretch revealed to me just how inhibited I was. Why couldn't I be free in my own skin? It helped to see that other women were equally squeamish. This wasn't a personal problem; it was a collective problem. No one in my past had ever informed me that I could trust my body, my sexuality, that it was to be honored and revered.

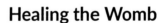

Nature Goddess

107

We learned how to give and receive positive touch on the third and final day. We did rituals of forgiveness and connected to the wisdom of the Great Mother. We were reminded that, like the earth, our bodies were sacred and needed to be treated in a sacred manner. But first, I had to learn how to fully inhabit my body.

After I left the retreat my friend and I spoke about it. We'd both been stretched much more than we could have imagined, yet I still did not feel I'd reached the core of what I was seeking.

Healing the Womb

How in the name of all that is holy, can anyone think that the place where all of us come from, the very place of our birth, is a place of shame?

~ Rufus C. Camphausen, *The Yoni: Sacred Symbol of Female Creative Power*

A few months later I came across an on-line class, Breaking the Grip of Past Lovers, by Jumana Sophia. Her course introduction, in part, was:

Even if you've made a million repetitive choices that seem in denial or outright abuse of your own right to respect and love,

Your woman's body (as it was created to be) is a magnificent, subtle, and beautiful living temple that thrives and responds with great grace to: devotion, respect, sensitivity,

And most importantly ...... your own loving, consciously directed attention and care.

Her words awakened something that I instinctively knew to be true.

My body was a sacred temple capable of bringing life into the world. It knew how to nourish and support life. How had I ever doubted that my body could be anything other than beautiful? How had I come to consider it as such a source of shame? How had we as a culture and religion gotten here?

As Jumana led me in meditations, taking me down into my womb, I felt my heart open in compassion for my young self. I was not a bad person. My body was not bad. My sexuality was not bad. I began to feel and truly understand what an honor it was to be a woman—to fully inhabit my body. I was no longer ashamed.

Throughout the course, Jumana also encouraged us to look at and own those instances when we had hurt others with our sexual choices. As much as I wanted to blame others, I had to admit that I had used others at times to assuage my own need for power and attention and I had not always fully honored or respected others in the process. I had manipulated others to get what I wanted.

Marion Woodman once said that if we had been tyrannized, we would tyrannize others or tyrannize our bodies. I didn't want to think of myself as that kind of person, yet I knew there were times when I had sliced-and-diced myself, my body, and my partner with my words. I was capable of demeaning others. Ouch! I had to admit that sometimes it felt safer to remain the victim than to grow up and take responsibility for what I had done.

I wish I had known a fully-embodied woman in my teens who could have taught me that my sexuality was beautiful, life-giving, and that my body was a sacred temple. Perhaps it would have saved me a lifetime of heartache. But the wounds and the desecration of the feminine (the sacredness of body and matter) runs deep in our political, religious, and cultural systems and it will be many years before those wounds can be fully acknowledged. We must be the ones to make conscious what has been denied; in doing so we create the change. To heal is to make holy. As we heal our sexuality, we connect life to its sacred core. We remember the earth, matter, and the Great Mother as sacred; we are nourished by her wisdom.

The Creative Life Source

We tend to associate sexual energy with sex, but sexual energy is the life force energy that moves through *everything*. When the body and soul are connected, the body is alive, the senses awakened. The Spanish have a term for this energy, duende, which means having a quality of passion, inspiration; spirit moving through the body. Think of flamenco dancers who know how to express through their bodies.

When a woman reconnects with her sexuality as an innate creative life force, she recognizes that it can take many forms as she expands her creative expression of her sexuality to include dance, poetry, art, or music. She understands that embracing her feminine sexuality allows her to have all her senses heightened, to be fully present in the moment, to experience her truth, and to feel complete. To be sexual as a woman is to be alive.

~ Anita Johnston, Ph.D., *Eating in the Light of the Moon: How Women Can Transform Their Relationships with Food Through Myths, Metaphors & Storytelling*

As we inhabit and love our bodies, they become clear channels for the divine to inspire and enliven all our senses; we connect to the sensual in all its aspects which can be expressed in many ways, including creativity.

Pleasure can be associated with more than sexual enjoyment or satisfaction; it can also be expressed through anything that brings us happiness, delight, or joy. Pleasure enlivens our senses and reminds us that we are a part of something larger – the sacred is always present in our lives. Our body and soul become quiet and are nourished by this presence.

Inhabit your body, follow what brings you joy!

Goddess of Fertility and Abundance

Inhabiting Our Bodies

We can only love others as well as we love ourselves.
~ Jan Phillips, *Divining the Body: Reclaim the Holiness of Your Physical Self*

When a woman follows those things that bring her joy and make her come alive she can't help but be a magnet to others. Before she can be a magnet to others, she must be comfortable in her own skin and believe she has a right to follow her passions.

My journey to re-inhabit my body started the moment I realized that my body was a sacred temple. This truth helped me see that I needed to be mindful of what I put into my body and who I invited in. Unfortunately, I didn't make that discovery until I was in my fifties and deeply scarred.

As I shared previously, I didn't realize that I deserved to be cherished. Yet we must first believe that we are worthy of love and respect if we want others to love, respect and cherish us. Women create and nurture life through their bodies so a loving connection with our bodies is important.

For many, separation from the body comes as a result of trauma and/or abuse, so be loving and tender with yourself as you embark on this part of your journey. Your task is to heal unresolved hurts of your past so that you and your body can become a vessel for life to happen in and through you. Life is erotic. Open your senses and allow the beauty of life to dance with you and in you!

Exercise 1 - Self-Reflection

Write about your initiation into womanhood in your journal. Were you supported when you started your menstrual cycle? Did your mother and/or father talk to you about sex? Were they open about being sexual? Were they able to acknowledge you as a sexual being? What was your early sexual history? Where are you at present with your sexuality? How do you see your sexual self? In what ways do you honor, respect/ disrespect your body, your sexuality? Drop any judgment that may arise and accept yourself wherever you are. You have done your best.

Exercise 2 - Come to Your Senses

Supplies:

° journal   ° watercolors

- At the top of five pages in your journal (paint them with watercolors, if you like), write: *"I give you the gift of..."*

- On each page, name one sense (smell, sight, sound, touch, taste), respectively, after the words *gift of.*

- Next, write down all the smells you love on the first page, and continue through the other senses – the beauty you have seen, the sounds that soothe you, the gifts of touch, tastes you love.

Refer to these pages often. They contain those things that feed your soul, awaken your sensual self, and bring you home to your body.

Spirit Companions

Exercise 3 - Love Your Animal Body!

You may find that listening to and paying attention to your pet is easier than attending to your own body.

- Listen: What if you were to listen to your body as if it, too, were a beloved pet? How would you move, play, rest? What kind of diet would you need?
- Connect: Learn to connect to your body by pausing throughout the day to connect with your breath. Put your hand on your heart, pat your chest and let your body know you are here.

- Assess: Do a quick body scan. Notice what you notice. Is there anything you could do to bring more love and comfort to yourself?
- Gratitude: Give gratitude to your body for all that it has done for you. Acknowledge the places it has carried you, how it has served you, the pain it has carried for you. Send your body love, gratitude, and appreciation. Notice that, like a beloved pet, it too responds to your attention. Write a letter of gratitude to your body.

For additional exploration ideas, go to my website (see page 6 for details).

Color-Filled

The Conscious Queen

To be yourself in a world that is constantly trying to make you somebody else is the greatest accomplishment.
~ Ralph Waldo Emerson

Most fairy tales end with the line, "The Prince and Princess were married and lived happily ever after." Psychologically what this means is that the energies of the opposites have come together; what has been fragmented has been united. The feminine path to wholeness joins the fragmented parts of the self and makes it whole.

Rarely do we get to live *happily ever after*, no matter how awesome our life is. That's why I like the ending of the modern-day movie of Cinderella titled, Ever After, which says, "It's not that they lived happily ever after, but that they lived!" The gift of this life-long search for my true self is that I get to be me. The shackles of the past no longer limit me, I have become the author and co-creator of my life. I get to be me, the me I was before society told me who to be. Being me is all I have ever wanted to be!

I am grateful for my life and for this journey, even though at times it has been arduous and painstaking. Just like the Velveteen Rabbit said, "You become. It takes a long time. That's why it doesn't happen often to people who break easily, or have sharp edges, or who must be carefully kept. Generally, by the time you are Real, most of your hair has been loved off, and your eyes drop out and you get loose in the joints and very shabby."

This year I turned 63 and most of my youthfulness has faded, but I wouldn't trade being real for anything. Everything that has happened in my life was in service to this moment; it was designed to bring me back to my true self and crown me with wisdom.

It has been a difficult journey, because it required that I let go of nearly everything I believed to be true. But that's how we become the conscious queens of our lives. We let go; we shed the old attitudes, the old beliefs, so something new can be born.

The beauty of life is that it is always calling us to wholeness. Every struggle, every hardship, every crisis is a signal calling us to our greatness, to our full potential. It is calling us to the life we were born to live...returning us to our original selves.

The life/death/rebirth cycle of life is the path of the feminine—life forever renewing itself; death in the service of life. Although its paradoxical nature takes us into grief and despair, its purpose is to restore us, to renew the light, for it is in our despair that we turn our faces to God. Life is always calling us back to our true selves.

You are the Wild, gorgeous, smart, playful, sensual, creative, beautiful, and strong woman that you are... because of, not in spite of, the experiences of your life.

~ Wild Woman Sisterhood

We cannot rediscover our true-selves until we are truly honest and face our dark places: those unloved, rejected, hidden, and abandoned parts of ourselves. It is in accepting both the light and the dark within ourselves, accepting the dualities of life, that we are made whole and our creativity is released.

In Full Bloom

Transformation requires that we love ourselves, warts and all, nothing less. As children, we depended on others for love, but it is now our task to be the one to love us. In loving ourselves, we become free. God does not withhold, we do!

As we open our hearts in compassion for ourselves, a beautiful thing happens: our hearts open to others who suffer, as well. When we heal our bodies and our sexuality, we hear the cries of the earth and all beings. It is in the heart where, above and below, spirit and matter meet and restore us to wholeness. Our suffering connects us with life and our shared humanity.

The Third Wave of the Feminist Movement

Maybe the journey isn't so much about becoming anything. Maybe it's about unbecoming everything that isn't really you, so that you can be who you were meant to be in the first place.

~ Summersaladana.com

I believe that women [and men] who are on their journey to wholeness, those who are becoming the heroines [heroes] of their own lives, constitute the third wave of the feminist movement. Many of us have been on this path for years; others are just beginning their journeys. Change begins with us, it begins in our willingness to: challenge the status quo, sit empty with our pain and sorrow, and let our lives crumble into the ashes as we await the resurrection so that we can come into the world anew. We become renewed as strong women, conscious queens, who are ready to stand in our truth, fully embodied and empowered.

Sisterhood

As I write this last chapter, I see a shift in our political and social climate - we have entered an era in which our rights as women are threatened once again. The Dali Lama said it is western women who will awaken the world. That is so because we have achieved a degree of economic stability. Many women have taken the journey to wholeness, healed their lives, and are ready to stand in their power and bring their gifts forward.

I attended the first Women's March in January 2017 along with so many people around the world. As we drove to the city, my friends and I talked about the women who had come before us, those who had fought for our rights. We felt such gratitude for their suffering and their gifts. We recognized that we would not be where we are today without their sacrifices and we were proud to step onto that same path to claim our space; to stand on their shoulders to create a world of connection where all people, all beings, and our planet are united, connected and protected.

The Great Mother

rights, racial equality, and freedom of religion. The web of connection, created by the powerful emergence of the feminine, holds everything securely in place—every thing, everyone, every creature. For the feminine is the Great Mother who brings life into the world and nurtures all beings.

Many women intuitively know this truth and they long to heal the world. I would like you to know that by transforming yourself, you are healing the world. When we heal, we are less fragmented - we become whole and in so doing, we make holy our stories. Carl Jung wrote that the future of the planet hangs by the thread of individual consciousness. When we heal the separations within ourselves, we heal the separations of the world.

Women have the power to determine the quality of life for future generations.

~ Age of Myth

In addition, we must speak out and bring forth our gifts in honor of the sacred feminine, the great mother. Marion Woodman said that there have been times when the feminine balance was on the verge of returning, but each time we backed away. We must now be resolute and determined in our work. We must not let this be a still-birth. We must all become mid-wives supporting and birthing each other into being, so that new life can be restored to our planet. This work is both dangerous and full of possibility, but I believe we, together, can create a new vision that is sustainable to all of life!

The feminine principle is inclusiveness. Its nature is to join that which has been severed. The Women's March was much more than a march for women. It provided a platform for rights for all. The 2017 Women's March was the largest ever single-day, global demonstration for human rights, women's rights, immigration reform, the environment, LGBTQ

Awaken the Masculine

We're so engaged in doing things to achieve purposes of outer value that we forget the inner value, the rapture that is associated with being alive, is what it is all about.

~ Joseph Campbell

In stories when life becomes imbalanced, the feminine wakes up the masculine and the masculine awakens the feminine; one does not overshadow

Standing in Her Power

the other but each supports the other. Our society has focused on power at the expense of love and on doing rather than being for too long. We have honored the intellect and overshadowed intuition. We have paid attention to spiritual goals yet detached from our bodies, matter, and the earth. As we heal ourselves, we bring all together. It is from this place of wholeness that we will engage with our partners, our workplace, and our world.

Once empowered, we will no longer be satisfied to accept the status quo. Having found our voices, we will speak out. We won't treat men as our enemy because we understand that they are wounded as well. For the same reason, we will refuse to accept the unacceptable. After we have worked with our shadow-side, we will no longer need to project our wounds onto others.

Our voices will be strong and come from a place of truth, love, and wholeness—from our embodied wisdom. Our determination will be fierce because we know the importance of our fight: human rights, women's rights, the earth, and all beings. We women are not seeking to rule the world, we are looking to bring the sacred, the soul, and equality back into the world. In fact, our journey does not make us more powerful economically, it makes us more creative and alive. It ignites the fire that can fuel our passions...and our dreams. It is a spiritual fire.

Many of our brothers have already joined us on this walk; the feminine has been awakened in them, too. They are spiritual warriors. They are not emasculated men - they are men who have also suffered and endured the wounds of the feminine. They have heard the cries of the earth. They too long for soul. They are not in search of power and greed but are in search of a world where all beings can live in harmony, one in which the earth herself can be protected. They are men in service to life and in service to the *great mother*.

In the laws of creation, the masculine principle is in service to the feminine because the feminine is closer to the unconscious, to the darkness where life comes into being. In clearing ourselves of the old energies, the old beliefs, we make room for the seeds of the new to emerge, new dreams to be heard.

> *As we embody our dreams,*
> *we become the eyes, ears,*
> *hands, and feet of archetypal*
> *mother and father guiding*
> *their sacred child, humanity,*
> *into maturity.*
>
> ~ Andrew Levitt, *The Inner Studio*

The task of the feminine is to go into the world as the hands and feet. We endure this work because we are called to do it because we must! We serve in this way because we know we will never be free until all beings are free.

The Gift

> *Once we believe in ourselves,*
> *we can risk curiosity, wonder,*
> *spontaneous delight, or any*
> *experience that reveals the*
> *human spirit.*
>
> ~ e. e. cummings

Joseph Campbell says it is our aliveness that heals the world. Aliveness is the gift we receive when we take our journey to wholeness. This book and my paintings seek to demonstrate this truth. My own journey brought me back to my authentic self, returned my child spirit, and filled me with joy and aliveness. My child spirit wants to create, paint and express! The child in us is creative.

The book that you now hold in your hands could only have been possible through the healing of the feminine and masculine principles within me. Both,

masculine and feminine, are necessary for creation. It is in this union, the coming together of opposites, that creation occurs. And it is possible for all of us!

The world needs your gifts. When you become the person you were born to be and you, in turn, share your unique gifts with the world, the world will change. I once saw a sign in an airport that read, "Women: the largest untapped resource of the world." The world needs you to be whole; it needs you to be healthy so you can share your gifts with humankind. The world needs you to complete your journey.

Your gifts are hidden in the wounds and the limitations of your past. Give yourself permission to drop the cloak of conformity so that you can step into your essential self. By its very nature, your true self is unfettered, spontaneous, loving, and caring. Let go of the burden of being perfect and, instead, seek to recapture the lost parts of yourself. The answers you need are within you.

> *The cave you fear to enter*
> *holds the treasure you*
> *seek.*
>
> ~ Joseph Campbell

Isn't it a relief to know that you don't have to be anyone other than who you are? Are you comforted to know that you don't have to be like someone else? Pursue those things that bring you joy and make you come alive! As Rumi said, "There are a thousand ways to kneel and kiss the ground." Do not let anyone or anything diminish the value of your uniqueness, including yourself!

As I look back on my journey, I can see that I was never alone. Every time I thought I'd come to the end of the world, I discovered I'd only come to the end of the world as I had known it. Life reached out to meet me as I took my next step. There were many times when I thought I was forgotten and abandoned, just like my little girl-self waiting for my mom at the kindergarten door. I now know that the divine feminine was always with me...even when I was unaware.

In following my heart, I found a home within myself. I found forgiveness, love, healing, and life. I found my creativity. I found myself and a connection with, not a separation from, the divine – both God and the Goddess. What greater gift could there possibly be?

The Labyrinth

In a labyrinth, one does not lose oneself; in a labyrinth, one finds oneself. In a labyrinth, one does not encounter the Minotaur, one encounters oneself.

~ Hermann Kern, *Through the Labyrinth: Designs and Meanings Over 5,000 Years*

If you have walked a labyrinth, which is a feminine symbol, you probably know that the path to the center is not linear. You meander in and out, here and there, yet you always move toward the center point as you follow the path. Once you reach the center, you wind your way back, carrying the treasure or the wisdom you gleaned out into the world.

Our own life's journey is like a walk of the labyrinth; entering the labyrinth is symbolic of going into our psyche. Each turn represents our response to obstacles we encounter. As we approach the center, we connect with the divine, the holy within us. But our journey is not over until we make our way out of the labyrinth and share our wisdom with the world. Even though our journey is ongoing, we are always whole. In sharing our wisdom and aliveness, we impact the world and make it easier for the women, men, and children who come after us.

Malei

Blessed is she [anyone] who knows who [he or] she really is and builds a place to live there.
~ Rumi

Now that you know the way...

find your wings

and take flight

as the beautiful woman

you've always

known yourself

to be

and become the conscious queen

who rules her kingdom

with love and kindness and equality for all

for it is in you, becoming you

that you will finally be free

and the kingdom will be transformed.

With Gratitude!

Colleen R. Russell

Messenger of Hope

Standing in Your Power

There is nothing more rare, nor more beautiful, than a woman being unapologetically herself; comfortable in her imperfect imperfection. To me, that is the essence of true beauty.

~ Steve Maraboli, *Unapologetically You: Reflections on Life and the Human Experience*

magnificent
adjective mag·ni·fi·cent/mægˈnɪfəsənt

Magnificent: beautiful, splendid, spectacular, impressive, glorious; exalted; exceptionally good; excellent.

In my imagination, a queen is a magnificent woman who has been through the fires of initiation and has emerged with a deeper love and understanding of not only her own humanity, but that of others. She is a woman who has faced the darkness in herself and can accept the darkness in others. She is a woman who has learned to shake off the shackles of conformity to become her own person, a woman who has learned to trust and speak her own truth. A queen is a woman who has discovered that she is enough because she is a child of the Creator and now seeks to live in service to the divine.

She is a woman who is married to the king within her, a well-developed masculine source who helps her manifest her creative ideas. She recognizes that she and her king have equal value and they work co-operatively to serve the greater whole. She knows who she is, what she values, and she expresses that in all that she does.

She is also aware that her growth is never complete. She chooses to spend equal amounts of time with the inner symbolic world and the outer world so she can hear the messages coming from within. She remembers her wholeness and at the same time continues to expand.

She is a woman who loves herself and is therefore capable of loving others. She can be fierce and courageous, when needed, and is able to cut away what is no longer of service, yet her foundation is always love.

Qualities of a Conscious Queen

- committed to knowing who she is
- possesses a deep acceptance of herself
- clear about her needs and wants
- true to herself
- searches for balance in all things
- comfortable in her own skin
- cares for her body
- asks for what she needs
- motivates and inspires others by her presence
- respects her true nature and all of nature, as well
- seeks justice
- expresses the creative life force within her
- accepts both the dark and light sides of life
- lives her creative dreams
- connects with both the inner and outer worlds, equally
- able to cut away the superficial

Ruler of Her Kingdom

Excercise 1 - Honoring Your Transformed Self

Supplies:

°2 pages card stock
°scissors
°glue
°patterned craft paper, paper

napkins, fabric scraps
°beads, cording, yarn
°markers, paints, colored pencils
°butterfly pattern

Download the pattern from my website (see page 6 for details) and print on card stock. The pattern consists of 3 parts on two separate pages - the body and two wings. Cut out. Next, glue the wings onto the body. Decorate the butterfly any way you'd like... color it with paints and markers, dress it with paper and fabric, and embellish it with beads and cording. Let your creative-self play; have fun!

Celebrate the work you've done in your transformation journey – spread your wings and fly!

Inspired Viewing
  Fabulous Fashionista at
  https://www.youtube.com/channel/UC3HOfMt63Mc5BDyxOutBv9w

A Music Reminder
  Be Yourself by Peruquois at https://www.youtube.com/watch?v=idq-Zw1VF5c

Afterword:

The tipping point is that magic moment when an idea, trend, or social behavior crosses a threshold, tips, and spreads like wildfire.
~ Malcolm Gladwell, *The Tipping pint, How Little Things Can Make a Big Difference*

We ended 2017 with, what felt like, a tipping point for women's rights as the power and fierceness of the #MeToo movement was unleashed. Corporations pulled advertising dollars to demonstrate their values of equality, and businesses fired top talent for sexual harassment and sexual assault allegations. The roar of the Goddess was loud and clear, "Enough! No more!"

The fall from grace of the power-filled masculine came at such a whirlwind pace that it was difficult to integrate. Questions remain unanswered: what constitutes abuse? and what are the consequences of those abuses? One thing we know, a new bar has been set and there are now life-changing consequences for the abuses of power and privilege that have been inflicted on women for centuries.

At times it has been difficult to witness the desecration of careers and lives of so many talented, powerful men – their lives changed forever. I am reminded, we do not come to consciousness without pain and a crisis moment is a wake-up call! The old masculine is being asked to wake-up and live from a more conscious place so that we might have both a conscious queen and a conscious king at the helm.

The possibility for deep change exists; we are at a pivotal moment. We must be cautious, however, because there is also danger.

I warn the reader not to expect a quick-fix. This behavior is pervasive in our history, psyches, workplaces, and homes; and it will take years to fully embody a new consciousness. There are many forces, internal and external, at work that do not want change. We must be patient, forthright, and vigilant.

The primary danger, as I see it, is that women's wrath will be awakened and women will seek destruction rather than transformation. Remember, we are called to seek equality and the inner marriage of the masculine and feminine principles, not power over or the exclusion of one or the other. The other dangers are that we 1) will become tired, complacent, and stop taking the steps required to ground the change, 2) will fail to see that the masculine (power principle or the old patriarch) resides in us too and will, therefore, collude with our perpetrators and hold the change at bay because of our outdated beliefs, 3) will judge others who have not yet come to consciousness which will increase the division, and 4) will endanger men's lives by making accusations before we fully understand what constitutes abuse which could cause retaliation and deflate the power of the #MeToo movement.

T.S. Elliott reminds us, "Without the still point there is no dance. And there is only the dance." Change is born through the tension of opposites. True power lies in each of us finding our still point so that we respond from that place.

Oprah Winfrey eloquently expressed in her acceptance of Golden Globe's Cecil B. DeMille Award in 2018 that, "... a new day is on the horizon," Many of us can feel it in our bones. We must hang on to that hope - let it fuel our imaginations, hold us accountable and allow us to forgive - and move forward into the possibilities of this new day.

I believe that the feminine path to wholeness holds the key to our re-imagination of a new horizon because what is needed is nothing less than total transformation!

Throne of Empowerment

Stay Connected

Visit My Website
Go to www.theartfulsage.com for a list of services, to access my Art Gallery and Storefront, subscribe to my newsletter, learn about upcoming events, and contact me.

Subscribe to My Free E-Newsletter
If you'd like to receive inspirational articles and notices of upcoming events delivered via email, please sign up for my monthly e-newsletter. Subscribe through my website at www. theartfulsage.com

Like My Facebook Page and Join My Facebook Group (same name as this book)
You can like my Facebook page from my website at www.theartfulsage.com. I share daily inspirational images, inspirational thoughts, and words of wisdom.

Send Me an E-Mail
Feel free to send me a personal e-mail at colleen@theartfulsage.com I would especially love to hear about your journey and your experience in reading this book.

Recommend to a Friend
If you liked this book, please post a review at www.amazonbooks.com. There are so many books available online and people depend upon the opinion and experience of others before buying. Your insight is invaluable.

Start a Book Study Group
Expand your community by sharing the book in a study group. It could make for interesting conversation.

Retreats
If you want to deepen your experience in your journey, join me for a woman's retreat. I offer weekend experiential women's retreats every spring and fall and co-facilitate women's adventures in Europe each summer with Alchemy Adventures.

Speaking Engagements
If you'd like to hire me to speak at an event on women's issues, spiritual transformations, life transitions, or creativity; please contact me for more information at colleen@theartfulsage. com

Thank you for your love and support!

Glossary

Conscious Queen: a woman who has been through the fires of transformation, knows who she is, and has become the author of her own life. She is able to stand in her power, speak her truth, and manifest her dreams. She is a woman who has healed and brought the opposites together within herself. She has learned to love and respect herself and is free.

dark night of the soul: a term that describes the void state often experienced after all the outer identities have been stripped and a person is without hope and dreams. It is a place where we feel abandoned, even by God.

Divine Feminine, Sacred Feminine, Goddess, Great Mother: names that represent the yin or feminine aspect of the godhead.

feminine path / feminine path to wholeness: represents the internal changes a person goes through as they move from an ego-based consciousness to become a whole self, which is to live with God or the transpersonal at the center rather than the ego. It is a process where a person becomes aware of all her personal strengths and weaknesses and accepts them all, living consciously from this empowered place, and becoming an agent of change in the world.

first wave of the feminist movement: gave women the right to vote.
second wave of the feminist movement: pushed for further equality, not just for women but for all people, protection from physical abuse, reproductive rights and more control over their own bodies, to be seen as more than just an object of beauty.
third wave of the feminist movement: has not been officially declared, but is what I call the deep inner transformational work women (individually and collectively) do to become conscious of who they are, discover the divine feminine, heal the wounds within, see and transform the old patriarch that lives within them, discover their uniqueness, learn to stand in their power, and speak their truth.

God, Higher Power, The Sacred, The Divine, power greater than yourself: names used to identify the source that created us and that is a part of our lives.

Handless Maiden: a mythical story of a woman coming into wholeness that reminds us of the endurance required of us.

power principle: using willpower to attain success, power, fame, or fortune at the expense of listening to the body, relationships, and the earth.

sacred marriage: a union of opposites (masculine and feminine).

shadow: the unconscious traits and attitude of a person, both negative and positive that the conscious mind has either ignored or rejected.

Made in the USA
Lexington, KY
04 December 2018